JUNIPERO SERRA, PIONEER OF THE CROSS

Recognized by the American Revolution Bicentennial Commission of California.

Junipero Serra, Pioneer of the Cross

by

Bernice Scott

Panorama West Books

Second Printing 1985

Panorama West Books
2002 N. Gateway, Suite 102
Fresno, California 93727

Library of Congress Catalog Card Number 75-27785
International Standard Book Number 0-914330-80-2

Manufactured in the United States of America

Preface

Father Junípero Serra, founder of the California mission system, was almost a legend in his own time. Although he was plagued throughout his entire life by a severely ulcerated leg and was never physically strong, his accomplishments approached the realm of the impossible.

The famed missionary arrived in Mexico in 1749 and for twenty years dedicated himself to the task of building missions and converting Indians. When, after these long years of service he was ordered to take charge of establishing the California missions, he is said to have replied, "I cannot go. I have too much to do here." But obedience was his vow so he went, only to become more dedicated than ever to his work.

To Serra there was only one valid reason for the settlement of California—Christianizing the natives. The political need for the move was of little significance to him. Should it be necessary he was ready and willing to join the long list of priests martyred in the new world as long as he was able to found even one mission. This fanatical zeal was to cause friction between Serra and the military commanders, but Serra's perseverance always won in the end.

Legends played a large part in Serra's life. So numerous and confused were they that it is often difficult, if not impossible, to separate fact from fiction. Certainly his known exploits were so outstanding in themselves that they are the very substance of which legends are born. The most famous of the stories about Serra is that of his long walk to California.

All historians do not accept this report as established fact. Hubert Howe Bancroft in Volume I of his *History of California* notes that Serra did walk to California. The late Herbert S. Bolton, in his class lectures, always insisted that Serra walked every step of the way. Maynard Geiger, curator of the Franciscan archives at Santa Barbara and a recognized authority on Serra's life, seems to feel that such a feat would have been impossible because it would have slowed the progress of the expedition, and that the military commander would not have permitted that.

Some attribute the story to a misinterpretation of the Spanish word *andar,* which can mean "to walk" but more often simply means "to travel." Others think that Father Palou, who was devoted to his superior, unwittingly exaggerated. Yet, if one considers Serra's dedication, determination, and attitude toward his ravaged body and pain, the legend does not seem so far-fetched. Moreover, though the foot healed, the leg ulcer did not, and perhaps it was less painful to walk than to have the sore leg rub against an animal travelling over exceedingly rough terrain. Too, it was customary for missionaries to walk. Since there is support for both views, the reader may decide for himself whether or not the story is based on fact or in an exaggeration on the part of Serra's admirers. Certainly no work on the life of Junípero Serra could omit it or fail to include the many other legends surrounding the great man.

Father Junípero Serra is one of the most popular figures in California history yet until this book there were relatively few easily-readable, accurate accounts of the life of the beloved mission founder. Most previous books offer more pleasure to the student and historian than to the young or general reader.

For the researcher there are the diaries and reports of contemporaries of Serra such as Crespi, Fages, Palou, and Costanso. Zephrin Engehardt's four-volume work *Missions and Missionaries of California* offers a wealth of detail on the building of the missions and the men who built them. Also, mission records are accessible. However, few of these works could be classified as popular reading.

Junipero Serra, Pioneer of the Cross must be classified as fiction, because, although the characters are historical figures, their conversations and the detailed description of events and things around them are the creations of the author. Miss Scott has kept closely to the historical data and the known legends, and the ideas, atmosphere and conversations are what might have been expected. Not only has the author retained historical accuracy, she has also brought long-gone historical figures back to life—warm, breathing, acting men.

There is an added attraction in *Junipero Serra, Pioneer of the Cross,* for Miss Scott writes with simplicity and charm. She has woven together the events in the life of Father Serra with warmth and affection. It is a book which should please persons from eight to eighty.

Gwendolin B. Cobb
August 10, 1975

Contents

I

A Day
In Petra

The first rosy streaks of morning touched a tiny stone house in the white-walled village of Petra, as a stalwart peasant lad limped hurriedly to the wooden door and banged his hand against it.

"Miguel, Miguel, I must talk to you. Come at once," he cried.

In a matter of minutes a small slender boy, but recently wakened from sleep, thrust his dark head out the door.

"What is it, Pedro? What brings you here at this hour?"

"You must do me a favor, Miguel. I stepped on my father's pruning knife last night and cut my foot. This morning I can hardly walk. I was to carry the Holy Cross in the procession to the church for this feast of our Blessed Mother. Do you think you can carry it for me, Miguel?"

"Oh yes," the smaller boy replied quickly, and joy was

1

in his soft voice and sleepy brown eyes. "I can carry it very steadily, I know."

"Is it to carry the crucifix, Pedro?" came the voice of Miguel's mother, hastily buttoning her peasant dress as she came from a back room. "But it is very heavy, and Miguel is so small. I fear he has not the strength." The mother looked from the robust, ruddy-cheeked Pedro to her own under-sized, frail son.

"But, Madreçita," protested Miguel, "it is our Lord I am to carry. I will be able to do it. God will give me strength—if I ask Him."

The mother saw the happiness in her boy's face as he closed his eyes tightly for the hasty prayer he was already offering to his Heavenly Father for strength to do his task.

"Very well," she said to Pedro in a low tone. "Miguel will bear the cross."

Margarita Serra well knew how her son's determination would overcome seemingly impossible obstacles. She knew, too, that his prayers always seemed to be answered, where those of others might be turned aside. She had spoken of this once to the good priest at the convent. The pious man had been thoughtful for a moment. Then he had answered, "Yes. Perhaps it is because he prays for the right things—never that his task be made easy; only that he be given the courage to perform it."

Yes, Miguel would carry the cross.

As the little procession made its way along the narrow street to the chapel of the convent of San Bernardino, the mother's heart ached as she and Miguel's father watched before entering for Mass. The cross, indeed, was borne steadily, never faltering as it rose high above the bright vestments of the priests and the black and white robes of the acolytes, for Miguel's head was pressed tightly against the wooden shaft. Great drops of perspiration glistened on his face as the hot Mediterranean

2

House where Father Serra was born in Petra.

sun beat down that day on the island of Majorca, off the coast of Spain. His feet stumbled against the uneven cobbles of the street. How could that simple peasant mother and father know, as they watched, what untold miles those feet would travel on the dusty trails of an unknown land to bring the Holy Cross and its message to a people they would never see.

Within the dim old church, as the service progressed, the voices of the priests and the boys they had trained to sing in the choir rose in the happy rejoicing of "Gloria in excelsis Deo," or fell in quiet adoration at the "Et homo factus est." Miguel was so short that he could not reach the choir rack before him, but his delicate oval face, upturned to the notes on the pages above him, was glowing with the joy he felt, and his voice came out true and golden.

After Mass, the good Franciscan padre, who was Miguel's teacher, came out of the church to talk to the parents. "Antonio," he said, placing his hand on the father's shoulder, "unless I am much mistaken, the small Miguel will one day be a scholar of the Church. His brilliant mind races along so fast that it will soon outstrip us here. We shall not be able to teach him any more. Then he must have a better teacher than this poor village padre."

"Surely, Padre, you joke," protested Antonio Serra. "Our Miguel is only a child, and so small for his age."

"Well, perhaps we can keep him busy here for a day or two longer," laughed the priest. "I think he is destined for the Church, though. His whole life is centered about this convent. The good God seems to have marked him for His own. Do not be surprised, either, if the boy wishes to join our order. He has never said so, and perhaps has not admitted it to himself, but I have reason to believe that Miguel would like to be a Franciscan."

The padre was remembering the glow that came to the boy's eyes whenever he had heard the stories of the life of St. Francis, which were often told the pupils of the convent school. As a young child in his first year in school, he had heard of the gentle Francis Bernardone, the rich young man who had lived five hundred years before in the town of Assisi, in Italy. One day the youth had decided to give up his life of wealth and pleasure, and to spend his time helping the poor and sick.

"I'd like to do that, too, when I am a man," Miguel had said.

As he had grown older, he had learned the stories by heart, and often told them to the younger children. That very day the padre had heard him telling a group of wide-eyed little boys the tale of Saint Francis and the wolf.

"The people of Gubbio, a town near Assisi, were afraid to go outside the walls of their town," he had begun, "for a fierce wolf had been terrifying the neighborhood.

4

Francis and two or three of his friends, who called themselves the 'Little Poor Men,' wanted to help the people of Gubbio. On the road they met a wolf, who charged toward them with jaws open, ready to spring. Now, Francis thought that, since all the animals and birds had been created by the same God who had made him, they were his brothers and sisters.

" 'Come here, Brother Wolf,' Francis began in a very calm voice. 'I ask you, for Christ's sake, to do no harm to me or anyone.'

"The wolf stopped running. He stared at this strange man, dressed in a long coarse robe, and slowly his jaws closed. Quietly, the beast lay down at Francis's feet, as he spoke to him again in his curious hushed voice.

" 'You have killed human beings, who are made in God's image. Because of this you deserve to be punished like the worst of murderers. Everybody here fears you and is your enemy. But I do not wish to harm you. I only want to make peace between you and the people of Gubbio.'

"In the dust of the road the wolf's head, body, and tail bobbed up and down, as if he agreed to this.

"Francis continued, 'Since you seem to have committed your crimes because you were hungry, I promise that the people will give you food. In return, you must promise never to harm any person or animal.'

"Francis held out his hand, and the wolf laid his paw in it.

"Now we shall go to the town square, where you must do this before all the people to show that you are sincere."

The once fierce beast walked meekly through the streets, and again put his paw in the Little Poor Man's hand. The people of Gubbio were delighted, and brought him food at once. From that day he lived in peace with all. When he died of old age, the townspeople mourned as if he had been a person."

Miguel had finished his story, and looked thoughtfully at the little boys. "I think the holy Saint Francis must have been very close to God, for the very beasts understood his words." Then he added, "His followers, the Franciscans, must be close to God, too."

Yes, Miguel Serra, with his quick mind and gentle ways, would almost surely find his way into the life of the Church, thought the padre.

"It would be wonderful to have our son in the Church," said the father, as the parents walked toward their home.

"Yes," breathed his wife. "Was it not, perhaps, for this that you brought him to be baptized on the very day of his birth?"

Antonio Serra thought of that blustery morning, the twenty-fourth of November in the year of 1713, when his fourth son had come into the world. The infant was so tiny and sickly that it was feared he would not live. Three other boys born to the Serras had failed to survive, and it looked very much as if the spark of life in this thin, tiny mite would go out before the child could be baptized. The father remembered how he had snatched up a blanket, wrapped the limp body in it, and run through the dark, sleeping village to the church.

"Baptize him quickly, Padre, before it is too late," he had pleaded when the priest had been aroused. "His name is to be Miguel José."

"Yes, since that day, it seems," he said, "our boy has loved the Heavenly Father and His Church."

Margarita Serra nodded.

After a minute Antonio went on slowly, in a half-ashamed voice, "But who will take care of us, Margarita, in our old age? There is only our little Juana. Our farmers' life is hard, and soon we shall not be able to work any more. Have you thought of that?"

"If the good God takes our only son for His work, I am

6

sure He will take care of us," she replied in the firmness of her faith.

"You are right, Margarita," nodded the father after a minute, "if the Lord wants him, the Lord shall have him."

Meanwhile, Miguel had watched the other boys playing for a time after Mass. As it was a feast day, there would be no lessons. The game of pelota was fast and rough, and Miguel tired too quickly to play very often. He wished, anyway, to translate a difficult passage in Latin that would be part of tomorrow's lesson. So, leaving the noise and heat of the courtyard, he went up to the classroom. How quiet it seemed! Miguel took his book to an arched window, where he could look across the red roofs to the line of almond trees and the bright green terraced vineyards that sloped away from the village, up, up to the blue above. He thought how the arch of the window framed the scene, and made it look like one of the pictures in the padre's study.

Soon, though, the boy had forgotten the scene, for he was intent on the Latin passage. The sound of the words pleased his ear, and since nobody was there to hear, he boomed them out full and clear. He liked to think of the Latin words as the grandfathers and great-grandfathers of so many of the words in his own musical Spanish language. The translation proved easier than he had expected, and by noon he had finished it.

Usually, lunch was just a bit of bread and cheese, taken at home with his mother and Juana, or with his father in the fields. Because this was a feast day, the father had not gone out to work.

After the simple meal with all his family together, and an hour's rest, Miguel and the other boys had prayers and religious instruction at the convent.

Then came the time of day that Miguel loved best, when the orange sun slipped behind the vine-covered hills, and the shadows were beginning to nestle in the valleys to drape the ridges with a soft purple veil. It was then that the Angelus called all the world from their duties, and bade them lift their hearts to the Creator. The boy fancied that even the bells were touched by the softening twilight, and their voice was warm and flowing. There was a hint of loneliness in it, too, and a beckoning note that seemed to speak to him of the future. "Far away," the notes sang to him as they grew dimmer and died away in the gentle air, "fa-ar, far a-way."

II
Student Days

One morning after Mass, the boys of Petra stood outside the church door.

"We must wait and say 'adiós' to Miguel," said his friend, Pedro.

"To think that the smallest one of all of us is to go to Palma to study at the university!" a broad-shouldered lad remarked. "Just imagine," he went on with awe, "he may even be a priest in time, and come back and preach to us."

The idea of little Miguel Serra standing in the big pulpit preaching to the grown-up people made them all laugh.

"*Ola*, he may have his books and lessons," one handsome dark boy put in. "I wouldn't want to study all the time, the way he does. I want to have some fun in life."

"Well, but Miguel is always happy," said another. "The padre says it is because he loves God so much."

Just then, Miguel himself, his father and mother, came out of the church door with the priest.

"Farewell, Miguel José," said the padre, laying his hand

on the boy's head, "may God bless you always."

"Adiós, Miguel," shouted the boys.

"Adiós, my friends, adiós," smiled the boy as he and his parents set out on the dusty road that led over the hills to Palma.

Not long before, the priest had reminded Antonio Serra of something he had told him a few years before. "The time has come," he said, "when we can teach Miguel no more here. His mind is like a hungry mouth, ever seeking more and more to fill it. It is not often that God gives such a desire to His children. It would be sinful not to fulfill it. He must go to Palma, where he can take higher courses, and perhaps later, even go to the great university itself."

So, at the age of fifteen, Miguel was on his way to become a real student. In appearance, he was still a child, for though the years had sped on, and his eager mind had raced ahead of them, his body had failed to keep pace.

Now, as he walked briskly along, with all his belongings in a bundle under one arm, his mind was a huge question mark. What would Palma be like? Would he be able to do as well as the other boys? Would they think him just a child, and laugh at him? Would he be thought worthy to join the Order of Saint Francis? This had come to be his great wish in life, though he had not dared to speak of it to anyone.

As he was thinking these thoughts, a large flock of birds made a black cloud as they rose from the branches of a twisted old fig tree at a bend in the road. Miguel smiled to himself as he thought of the story of the gentle Saint Francis preaching a roadside sermon to the birds, whom he called his sisters. According to the story, the birds had stayed quite still and listened devoutly. The boy wondered if the day would ever come when he, too, might be a great preacher. He put the thought aside, though, quickly, as being sinful, and blushed with shame at the idea of even thinking of himself in the same role as the revered saint.

As the travelers came into the "Golden City" of Palma, Miguel's doubts and fears returned. There were so many people! Surely the life of a boy from the country might well be swallowed up among so many. Just then, his father pointed out the tower of the cathedral. For almost five centuries, he told the lad, it had risen above the roofs of the city. As Miguel looked, it seemed to him that it pointed straight to Heaven. In an instant his fears were gone, and he knew that here in this place, where a lifted finger of stone ever drew the eye and mind to the things above, he would be able to prepare himself for the life he hoped to lead in God's service.

It was not so easy, however, to adjust himself to his new life. The padre at Petra had arranged for him to live in the home of a priest of the cathedral, while he studied at the Convent of San Francisco. From the moment this fine man had ushered Miguel into his home, he was kindness itself, but this did not prevent the terrors of homesickness from clutching at the boy's heart. Almost from the instant he had watched the forlorn figures of his mother and father starting back to Petra, the waves of loneliness had begun to sweep over him. Day after day, when his lessons were over and the hush of twilight fell on the city beside the shining waters of the bay, he would be engulfed by the memories of his home. In his mind's eye he could see his mother ladling out the good thick soup to be eaten with chunks of dark bread for the evening meal. Pictures of his sister, Juana, playing with the cat in their tiny courtyard, and his father dozing in the doorway in the cool of the evening rose to taunt him.

So profound was the power of this feeling, that he began to dread the hour of the Angelus, which he had once so loved. It was only by falling to his knees on the stone floor of his small, bare room each evening, and praying for strength to overcome it, that the force of the spells of loneliness was gradually lessened. He was never to forget those evenings, though, and the dread of loneliness remained with him always.

He plunged into his studies, desperately at first, to relieve the loneliness, and then with the wonder and joy that learning had always held for him. His classes in philosophy, where he met the great minds of the past, and discovered their ideas of the meaning of life, were like a never-ending adventure to him. Theology, too, which taught the beliefs of the Church, held much delight for him.

He studied constantly, and his teachers, at first surprised that the country boy outshone all the other students, soon began to predict a brilliant future for him. "The small one from Petra," they would say to one another, "has become our finest student. He is going to be one of the great scholars of our day."

Strangely enough, though he loved his life of study, he did not seem to care about becoming a famous scholar. There was only one thing he wanted now, and that was to wear the robe of a follower of Saint Francis. He had confided his wish to the priest with whom he lived, and, to Miguel's surprise, the good man had encouraged him in it.

One day, when he had been in Palma almost two years, the padre said to him, "My son, the Reverend Father Perelló, Provincial (Superior) of the Franciscan Order, is coming to the convent soon. Make known your desire to him, if you wish it so much."

For the next few days Miguel could think of little else, and when the Provincial arrived, was taken by his friend to meet him. Father Perelló was walking up and down in the cloister garden, reading the daily prayers of his Office.

While he waited for the prayers to be finished, Miguel's moist hands were clasped behind his back, and he felt sure that his tongue would not move when it was time to speak. Finally, when the book of prayers was closed, Miguel crept up to the great man, and was presented to him.

"This is one of our most industrious students, Reverend Father," said Miguel's friend, the priest. "He has a request to make of you, and since it is a personal matter, I shall leave you alone."

"Well, my son?" began Father Perelló kindly, as Miguel stood and stared at him, seeming unable to speak.

Then, in a moment, the words rushed out, not as he had planned, at all. "I want to be a Franciscan, Reverend Father," he blurted out, and added, "right away."

The older man barely hid a smile as he looked over the childish form in front of him.

"In due time, my son," he agreed, "perhaps you can 'take the robe'. It is a hard life, though, and not for a child. You must grow a bit first, and then we shall talk about it."

Hot, bitter tears squeezed themselves out of young Serra's eyelids and slid down his burning face. Impatiently he wiped them away with the back of his hand, and then turned and ran from the garden.

Would this shame of being undersized never leave him? Must he give up this most desired thing in life simply because he had not grown as other boys did?

Miguel felt that he could not stay in the convent walls where this terrible disappointment had come to him. He bolted into the street, and began walking as fast as he could toward nowhere in particular. He saw no one as he hastened on, while the passersby in the street turned to look at the lad who brushed past them, staring straight ahead. How long he walked, he never knew, but at length he became aware of the cathedral walls towering above

13

him. Then he began, with shame, to realize that he had been, indeed, acting like the child he was thought to be. What he should have done was to come here in the first place, to the house of God, and ask for His help. Was his faith so weak that he had thought the Heavenly Father would forsake him at the very moment he wished to give his life to Him? Thankfully, then, Miguel fell on his knees in the dim cathedral, and the peace of prayer came over him.

As he came out of the church door, his guardian met him. "Where have you been, Miguel? I have been looking everywhere for you. Reverend Father Perelló told me what he had said to you, and I knew how disappointed you would be. He did not know, of course, that you are almost seventeen, and old enough, according to the rules of the Order, to take the habit. As soon as I told him, he reversed his decision. Soon, my son, you will be admitted to the Holy Order."

On the fourteenth of September in the year 1730 at the Convent of Jesus, outside the walls of the city, Miguel Serra put on the robe and cowl (hood), tied the rope cord with its hanging rosary about his waist, and stepped into the sandals of a Franciscan.

He was called a novice now, and the first year, or novitiate, would be a year of trial, in which he would prepare himself to take his final vows, and to decide, definitely, that he wanted to follow the religious life.

All the novices were required to do some work about the convent each day, but on the first day of his novitiate, the Master of Novices called Miguel to his office.

"My son," he began, "the Lord has not seen fit to give you a strong and robust body, like the others. Therefore, we shall not force you to labor as the others must do, for fear it might do you an injury. Instead, it shall be your duty to serve Mass each day in the chapel."

Much as he hated being smaller than others of his age, for once he was secretly glad of his size. Nothing could have pleased him more than being on the altar, close to our Lord in the Blessed Sacrament. He felt that it gave him strength and courage for each day's tasks.

His mind was still filled with his study of philosophy and theology, but the books that appealed most to his heart at this time were those telling of the lives of the saints.

Often one of the novices would say, "Miguel, tell us the story of one of the saints of our Holy Order. It is better to hear you tell the stories than to read them ourselves."

Then, in his fine, moving voice, he would recount vividly and with freshness every detail which he had stored in his amazing memory.

When the story was done, someone would always say, "I feel as if I knew that man—as if he lived right here with us."

The stories had a marked effect on others, but they inspired Miguel most of all. The ones which had the greatest appeal for him were those of the missionary frairs, like San Francisco Solano, Apostle of the Indies. He was a young Spanish Franciscan who had left his own land, and gone to the Spanish colonies in South America to work with the natives there, and teach them the ways of civilization and of God.

Gradually, as Miguel read and repeated the happenings in the lives of these brave men, there was born the wish to do as they had done. What a wonderful thing it would be to bring the knowledge of God's love to these heathens across the seas!

He had read somewhere that the Indians were simple and trusting, like children. How rewarding it would be to lead these simple minds in the way of truth.

It troubled him, too, to know that the first Spaniards who had gone to the New World—explorers and soldiers—

had been cruel to the Indians, even killing them and stealing their treasure. It was done for "the glory of Spain," the conquerors had said. What honor was there in cruelty, murder, and theft, Miguel often wondered. How much more glorious it was for his well-loved country to bring the blessings of brotherly love, of peace, and of knowledge of the truth to these simple people! It was men like the brave missionary frairs who were working for the real glory of Spain. Miguel Serra resolved in his heart to be one of them.

There was one fabulous name that appealed to him particularly, as he read of the Spanish colonies in the New World. California! Somehow, it seemed to sum up the romance of the distant lands. Perhaps, he thought, he might be sent to work in that far-off spot some day.

As the end of his novitiate year drew near, Miguel was perplexed by the matter of the name he should assume when he took his final vows as a Franciscan. At that time, when he "made his profession," he would take a name of his own choosing, by which he would be known for the rest of his life. "It must be a name which has some meaning for me—some significance," he would say to himself.

One of the early Franciscans who appealed most to Miguel was named Junípero, meaning the juniper tree. He was one of the little band of followers of Saint Francis himself, a jolly fellow, who was always playing tricks, and full of witty sayings. His love for the poor was so great, though, that he would give away to beggars all the food the brothers had. Once he even tried to take the gold lace from the altar cloth to sell it to buy food for the poor. He was devoted to his leader, Saint Francis, and stayed near him always.

"I wish earnestly always to be close to the gentle Saint Francis and his rule, too," Miguel told himself. "I shall be a second Junípero."

III

Teaching
and
Preaching
in Palma

On September 15, 1731, Miguel José Serra became Fray
(Brother) Junípero Serra. As he stood before the altar in
the chapel of the Convent of Jesus, and took his vows to
feed the hungry, clothe the naked, to live in poverty, and
to obey the rules of the Order of Saint Francis, tears of joy
came to his eyes. This was the day toward which most of
his life so far seemed to point. It was the day to which he
was to look back in the years to come, as the greatest one
of his life. "All good things came to me with the coming
of this," he used to say later, when he spoke of taking
his vows.

One of these good things was noticed some time later
by the priest who had been his guardian when Junípero
had first come to Palma. As they met on the street one
day, the older man looked at the young brother closely,

and said, with a smile, "Do I imagine it, or does our 'juniper' lift his branches closer to the clouds these days?"

Fray Junípero started in happy surprise. His life of late had been so full that he had not had time to think much about his size.

"Are you serious? Do you really think I'm growing taller?" he asked unbelievingly.

The padre chuckled, and looked down. "Either that, or Franciscan robes are shorter these days," he bantered.

Fray Junípero glanced downward, too. The gray cloth, which had once brushed his instep, was now well above his ankle. He could hardly wait to get back to his cell-like room at the convent so that he could measure. Yes, it was really true! At the age of eighteen he had begun to grow taller, at last.

As time went on, several inches were added, and when his full growth was reached, he was a man of medium height and size.

Soon after taking his vows, Fray Junípero was sent to the most important convent of Palma to continue his study of philosophy and theology. He mastered the courses so quickly that before long he was a teacher instead of a student. This convent made him a Lecturer of Philosophy, and he taught classes there for three years. He was such a brilliant, interesting lecturer that students began to flock to his classes.

The famous Lullian University granted him a degree in philosophy, and later one in theology, even before he was ordained a priest.

Padre Serra, as he was known after being ordained, became more and more well known as a professor, but his greatest fame came as a preacher. People of high and low estate came in crowds to hear him. Rich Majorcans and those in the upper ranks of the Church admired his sermons because of their brilliance and learning; the poor

Parish church of Petra.

and lowly liked them for their simple, steadfast faith, and because the man who gave them had chosen to share their poverty.

Each time that Padre Serra mounted the pulpit and saw the sea of faces staring expectantly up at him, he felt unequal to the task before him. These people—fishermen and sailors, priests and noble ladies, peasants and shopkeepers—were waiting to hear him say something that would make their lives better and holier. God expected him to win at least a few to the way of saintliness. Would he be able to say the right thing in a way that would do it? With the Lord's help, perhaps. So, for just a second he would close his eyes tightly, as he had done when a child, and pray.

Then, as he began to talk, and looked into those faces again, he felt the changes that came over them. He was reminded of flower buds in the spring. Tightly folded at first, they opened bit by bit to the warmth of the sun and purity of the dew. It seemed to him that the faces turned toward his own, and the hearts which were hidden, were opening in the same way to the words which told of the warmth of God's love, and the purity of His truth.

It was, indeed, true that he was a successful preacher. If proof were needed, it was to be found in his being asked to speak at the Lullian University on the anniversary of Ramón Lull, a famous poet and missionary, for whom it was named. It was a great feast day with all the scholars of the city there. The speech was in praise of the distinguished man's life. When it was finished, one of the best-known professors said, "This sermon is worthy of being printed in letters of gold."

The country boy from Petra stood on the peak of fame, but his soul was not satisfied. He thought again and again of the resolution he had made during his novitiate to become a missionary among the Indians of the New World. It grieved him to think that while he was surrounded by fame and honors in Palma, many of his "brown brothers," as he thought of them, roamed the wilderness never having heard of God's name.

The call to become a teacher of these heathens came to him loud and clear, and he made up his mind to answer it. He knew that the life would be one of untold hardships, but he was ready to shed his blood, even to become a martyr as others before him, in order to take the story of the cross to the brown, childlike people beyond the seas. Though he could not know it, the moment was to come soon when it seemed that a martyr's fate would be his, indeed.

Padre Serra found himself willing to die for his faith, if need be, but he was not prepared to meet a ghost of the past that rose to trouble him. One dismal Sunday he had been thinking about the new life he had determined to undertake. It was a day when dripping fog shut the island of Majorca off from the rest of the world. When the convent bells rang for the evening service in a muffled, unearthly voice, chill fingers gripped at Junípero's heart, and an old fear surged over him. It was the dread that had come to him with the notes of the Angelus years ago when, as a homesick boy, he had spent his first weeks in Palma. Then it had been actual loneliness of the present; now it was anxiety for the loneliness of the future. Taking up the life of a missionary would mean leaving all his friends—his brother Franciscans, his students and the other professors. It would mean, also, giving up the world of books, which the libraries of Palma offered him. He could bear even this, he thought, if there were someone to share his exile. The idea of going entirely alone, though, of being so far from his friends, cast a cloak of gloom over him.

Help from even this dread of loneliness, he believed, would be given him if he but asked for it earnestly enough. Here he felt the need to have someone more powerful than himself intercede for him. He decided to ask the Blessed Mother and San Francisco Solano to join him in asking the Heavenly Father to touch the heart of someone else with the wish to go as a missionary, also. For this purpose he made novenas (nine days of prayers), one to each of them.

The night after he had finished his novenas, Junípero went to see one of his favorite students and closest friends, a Franciscan like himself, named Francisco Palou. As soon as he entered the room, Padre Serra noticed a strange new light in his friends's eyes. He appeared excited, and said at once, "I have long been thinking of taking an important step in life. The time has come for me to decide, but I wanted to ask your advice first, Reverend Father. Will you give it to me?"

"Of course I will give it gladly," answered Junípero. "What is this step you are about to take?"

"I wish to go as a missionary to the natives of the New World."

Junípero could hardly believe what he heard. He jumped to his feet, and tears of joy were in his eyes. "I, too, have been anxious to go on this missionary journey. I have hesitated because there was no one to go with me as a companion, though I had not given it up because of that. As a matter of fact, I came here tonight to ask you to accompany me. There is no doubt in my mind that it is the Will of God that we go together. Still, we must pray earnestly for Heaven's guidance, and keep the matter between us."

Junípero well knew that his superiors at the convent and the university would try to persuade him not to go, if they heard of his intentions. They would tell him that he was too valuable in Majorca, that he had too important a career ahead of him to give it all up for the heathens across the seas.

Secretly, then, he wrote to the Commissioner General of the Franciscan Order for the "license" that he must have in order to go to America. The reply was very discouraging. It said that enough friars to staff the missions had already been chosen, and that they would soon leave. However, it promised to keep the request in mind, and hinted that it might be easier to get the "license" if he lived on the mainland of Spain.

Junípero at once asked to be sent to a college in Spain, but before an answer could be received, the Lenten season had come, and he was sent to preach in his native village of Petra.

Petra! How small the village seemed. The Church of San Bernardino, where as a child, he had stood on tiptoe to read the notes of music on the choir rack, had been enormous to him then. Now it looked like any convent church. His home, which to the small boy had been long and spacious, now seemed low and tiny. The very hillsides, whose slopes had shut out the rest of the world, appeared to have shrunk. How small everything looked, and how dear—doubly dear—for Junípero realized that he was seeing it all for, perhaps, the last time.

His old friends and neighbors filled the church whenever he preached, and they all felt as if a special sort of grace enfolded them during that Lenten season.

The evening of Palm Sunday, Junípero was walking in front of the convent when he saw, in the purpling twilight, a familiar figure approaching along the road. Francisco Palou!

"Welcome, Francisco," he shouted, "do you bring news?"

In answer, Francisco withdrew a letter from beneath his robe, and handed it to his friend.

"The license!" exclaimed Junípero, his voice filled with joy and excitement. "When did it come?"

"Today, just before the blessing of the palms," answered Francisco. "But I must tell you, Junípero, that it is not the first one that has come."

"What do you mean?"

"One of the brothers told me that a letter had been delivered before, but it was never given to me. This one came by special messenger."

"They do not want you to go, Fray," said his friend. "You are too fine a scholar, they say, to bury yourself in the wilds of New Spain. You should stay, they think, and continue to bring glory to the University. Someone tried to keep you from getting the letter."

Junípero was silent for a long minute. "It doesn't seem possible," he said thoughtfully, as a shadow came over his eyes. Then his face brightened, and he went on, "But

23

the important thing is that we have it, at last."

"Yes," agreed Francisco, "and we can leave as soon as possible."

"I prefer to remain here in my old home until after Easter," said Junípero. "In the meantime, you can return to Palma, and try to find a ship going to Cádiz. Mind that no one knows what you and I are about, though, or our secret will leak out."

Francisco agreed, and hurried back to Palma.

To Junípero Serra, Easter that year was the most joyous he had ever known, and at the same time, the saddest. It marked the beginning of a new, much longed-for chapter in his life, but it also brought to an end forever, the days of his childhood and youth in his beloved Majorca.

On the morning of his departure, he roamed through his old home, gazing lovingly at a few objects that would never leave his memory—the rosary hanging beside his parents' bed, an old doll of Juana's, dressed in blue "like our Blessed Lady," the waxy blossoms of the orange tree, whose perfume drifted through the courtyard.

Outside the door, he asked his parents' blessing for the work he was to undertake (though he did not tell them what it was), and knelt in the dust to receive it. Then he rose hastily, and without a backward glance, set out on the road to Palma, as he had done more than twenty years before, when he had first left Petra.

IV

The Voyage to the New World

Junípero stood on the deck of the small English ship that was to take him and Francisco Palou to Málaga, a port of southern Spain, from where they would sail to Cádiz. The friar's robes rippled about his ankles in the slight breeze that rose from the sparkling waters of the Mediterranean. With misty eyes, he watched the castle-crowned, rocky coast of his native island fade into the distance, with the cathedral spire pointing ever upward toward Heaven.

"Farewell, Majorca, land of my childhood. I shall never see you again," murmured Junípero.

His long, strong fingers touched the wooden cross that rested over his heart beneath his robes. It was the only possession he was taking with him on this journey half around the world.

Francisco Palou quietly joined him at the rail, and the

25

two friends watched until the island was just a dot in the boundless waters about their ship. Junípero was wiping his spectacles when a harsh, loud voice came to them from the deck.

"Gray robes!" it sneered, in English. "Mark my words, no good will come of this voyage, with them on board. But I'll put them in their place, never fear."

The Franciscans turned, to see the hulking, bearded captain talking to his first mate. They could not understand the English words he used, but the tone made the meaning clear.

"Do you think," Junípero asked his friend, "our captain does not care for our costume?"

"Neither the costume, nor what is inside it, I imagine, from the sound of his voice," answered Francisco.

The captain lumbered across the deck with an evil gleam in his eye, and asked the friars, in very bad Portuguese (since he spoke no Spanish), if they knew what the Bible had to say about a certain question.

Junípero at once began to quote the New Testament, but he had not gone far when the man interrupted him angrily, "That's not so. The Bible says something entirely different, and I can prove it to you."

"How?" asked Junípero quietly.

"Boy!" bellowed the captain to one of the crew. "Fetch my Bible. I'll show you a verse that proves you are wrong," he promised the friars.

The book, printed in English, was a massive volume with a heavy gold clasp. When it was opened, a musty odor that its many years at sea had imprisoned within its pages, came forth. With slow, deliberate movements, and much wetting of a huge thumb, the captain turned page after page, as a foreboding scowl appeared on his face.

"Can't find it just at this moment," he admitted

finally, "but I know it is there somewhere."

Again and again this happened, and always Junípero, who knew the Scriptures almost by heart, confounded the captain, who still stubbornly insisted that he just couldn't find the verse that would prove him right. One time, when the friar had the better of the argument, the captain vowed, in a leaping rage, that someone had torn a page from his Bible—the page he was seeking. Unable to control his anger, he shouted, "I'll pitch both you gray robes overboard, and sail for London."

He might have done so, too, except that Fray Francisco pointed out that they had passports signed by the captain himself, and if he failed to deliver them safely at Málaga, the King of Spain would demand satisfaction from the English government. The troublesome captain would then surely pay the penalty by losing his head.

Even this threat was not enough to force the man to hold his temper. One night, as usual, he had lured Fray Junípero into an argument. He became so enraged when the friar had clinched it beyond question with a perfectly remembered quotation, that he whipped out a dagger, which he thrust at Junípero's throat.

Startled as he was, Fray Junípero did not cringe or turn aside. "Perhaps," he thought, "this is the martyrdom the Lord has in mind for me. If so, I shall meet it bravely. But I hope it is not. I should hate to die before my missionary life has even begun, and I have had a chance to bring the word of God to my 'brown brothers' in the New World."

The raging captain quailed under the steady gaze of the courageous padre. He dropped his dagger, and shut himself up in his cabin for several hours. Junípero and his friend watched all night lest the captain return and carry out his threat. In the morning, though, his anger seemed to have left him, and the remainder of the voyage was

27

more or less peaceful.

The voyage to Málaga took two weeks, and after a stay there of five days, the friars took a coastal sailing ship for Cádiz. As soon as they arrived there, where other young men who were going as missionaries were gathered, they were taken to the Franciscan convent. Here they heard the story of how they had been chosen to go as missionaries to New Spain.

The friendly Commissioner of the Order of Saint Francis told them, "There were originally thirty-three friars from all parts of Spain. Some of them came from inland places, and had never seen or heard the ocean. A storm was brewing at the time. When some of the young men saw the huge gray waves battering the coast, and heard their mighty roar, they were terrified. Five were so frightened, they gave up their purpose to sail across the seas, and went back home. I was glad I knew from your letters where I could find at least two who were eager to take their places, I only wish," the Commissioner went on, "that there had been five of you."

Father Junípero at once spoke up, "We know of three others from Majorca who would like to come. If there is time, they can be sent for even now. I know they will leave everything, and come."

"There will be ample time, Father, for the missionaries are to be sent in two groups. Your friends may go with the second group. What are their names?"

Junípero Serra looked at Francisco Palou. "I know that my old school friend, Juan Crespi, would like to go," said Francisco.

"There are two others, Rafael Verger and Guillermo Vicens," put in Junípero, "who have been eager to become missionaries, too."

"Very good," beamed the Commissioner. "We shall send their licenses at once."

The two were overjoyed to know that three of their friends from Majorca would one day be with them.

Junípero would have liked to embark at once, but it was more than three months before their ship was ready to sail for the New World with the first group. Junípero and Francisco were in this group, which numbered twenty-one altogether. They left on August 28th in the year 1749, but they did not reach their destination, the port of Vera Cruz in Mexico, for ninety-nine long days.

The ship, a small one, pitched and tossed in the heavy seas. There were not only the Franciscans, but some other missionaries of the Dominican Order, as well as other passengers aboard. The cabin space was so small that there was scarcely room to stretch out to sleep at night.

When they had been more than a month at sea, and fifteen days from Puerto Rico, they began to run out of fresh water. One day this notice was put up for all to read:

"From this day forth, it will be necessary to ration the amount of water used by passengers of this vessel. The amount of one quart will be issued to every passenger each day. It is further necessary to forbid the making of chocolate for use as a beverage. These rules will be in effect until the island of Puerto Rico is reached."

Only four cups of water a day! The ship buzzed with the complaints of the passengers.

"I cannot open my eyes in the morning until I have washed with cool water," stated one of the friars. "If I use the water for that, there will not be enough left to quench my thirst during the day."

"In the heat of the tropics we shall die of thirst if we have no more water to drink than this," complained another.

"Ever since I can remember, I have had chocolate at least three times a day," remarked a lay passenger. "Now

I cannot have it even once. It is very difficult."

So the talk went on, and as day followed day, the murmuring grew louder. Only Junípero Serra seemed unmindful of the discomfort. One day one of his fellow missionaries blurted out, "I, for one, can't stand this torture much longer. How is it that you do not complain? Are you never tormented by thirst?"

"I have found a good remedy against feeling thirsty; and that is to eat little," — he glanced at the other friar, and went on with a twinkle in his eye, "to talk less, and so I save my saliva."

It was during this part of the voyage that Junípero came to feel, in a special way, the power and beauty of the sea. All his life, in his island home, he had been surrounded by its waters, but he had taken it for granted. Now, with its great expanse all about him, the tremendous unexplained energy of its throbbing waves came to have a new meaning for him. He thought of it as a symbol of the heart of the Creator, beating always for His creatures. When he was told that a certain place in the ocean was so deep that it had never been measured, he thought how like God's love for us. When a scarlet sunset turned the water to flame, or when, on a moonless night, a ribbon of phosphorescence trailed in the ship's wake, he was reminded of that love burning for even the most unworthy of people.

A warm peace and satisfaction would settle over his mind with the thoughts, for he felt that in taking up the missionary life, he had chosen well. Surely the "brown brothers" to whom he was going were as dear to the heart of the Almighty as any other of His children. How glad Junípero was that he had decided to give his life to bringing a knowledge of God to them. Even when, later on, the sea showed itself in an angry mood, his joy in it did not lessen.

After a fortnight's stay at Puerto Rico, where enough water for the rest of the trip was taken aboard, the little ship set sail on November 2, for Vera Cruz.

One month later, on a windy, threatening day, land was sighted, and the voyagers thought that their journey was almost over. Such was not the case, however, for when the ship was about to enter the harbor of Vera Cruz, the storm which had been blowing up all day, broke in fury about them. Unable to make headway against the raging winds, the ship was blown out to sea again, and took a northward course.

At the end of the day, the storm abated, only to be followed by a more furious one the next morning. Huge waves like liquid mountains rose over the decks with a deafening roar, and knocked the little craft about as if it were a toy. By the second night, the wind and waves were so fierce that all on board gave themselves up for lost. Terror clutched at the passengers. Padre Serra alone appeared quiet and serene.

"Are you not afraid, Junípero?" his companions asked him.

"I do indeed fear," he replied, "but when I remember what it is that is bringing me to the New World, I can put fear aside."

That night, when all the missionaries, both Franciscan and Dominican, were gathered in the cabin, a terrified boy dashed in. Shouting above the roar of the sea, he gasped out one dread word: "Mutiny!"

"What do you mean, boy?" the friars implored, crowding around him.

"The pumps won't keep out the water. The vessel cannot stand the strain much longer. The crew want to beach her so that some may be saved. They refuse to obey the captain and pilot."

The horror-stricken lad raced out, and the friars began,

31

with one accord, to prepare for the end. It was decided that they should all appeal to the Blessed Mother and to one of their patron saints, asking them to intercede for the helpless ship and its doomed passengers. Lots were cast, and the martyr, Santa Bárbara, was chosen. This was natural, since it was December 4, her feast day, and since she is the special patron saint of the storm-tossed. Too, she is one of the saints to whom the Order of Saint Francis have a special devotion.

As soon as her name was read from the lots, the friars with one accord shouted "Viva Santa Bárbara!"

Hardly had the sound of their voices ceased, when the winds began to lessen, the rain stopped, and the seas became calmer. The ship was able to turn south again, and within two days had anchored at Vera Cruz.

So it was that California's pioneer of the cross first came to the shores of the New World.

V
The Journey to Mexico City

The "klop-klop" of hoofbeats broke the hot afternoon quiet at the Franciscan Convent of Vera Cruz, where the missionaries were resting after their voyage. In through the high stone gateway trooped a score or more of horses and mules led by a Mexican on horseback, wearing a tremendous sombrero. Bringing up the rear were several heavily laden carts.

The leader dismounted and swept off his great hat as the Father Guardian, followed by most of the other friars, came to meet him.

"Your Reverence, here are the beasts which are to carry the missionary friars to Mexico City. The Viceroy sends them and the supplies in the name of the King of Spain," and he bowed, sweeping the ground with his sombrero again.

"Many thanks, sir," said the Father Guardian, bowing slightly.

The Mexican then drew near the priest, and covering his mouth with his hat, said in a low voice, "I brought the two extra mules, as you suggested, Padre."

"Thanks again," returned the Father Guardian. "If they are not needed, we shall send them back."

Bowing, the Mexican put on his hat, and mounted his horse. "The mule boys will remain," he said as he rode through the convent gates.

Meanwhile, the courtyard buzzed as the friars excitedly examined the animals. Soon each had chosen the one he would ride on the journey to the capital. Only Fray Junípero Serra and another younger missionary stood quietly in the shady arcade of the courtyard.

The Father Guardian approached them, and said to Junípero, "Are you still determined to walk, Padre?"

"Yes, indeed. I am well and strong, and I mean to carry out the orders of our Father, Saint Francis, and make my missionary journeys on foot," he replied firmly.

"When our Father, Saint Francis, gave that order, he was talking about the smaller countries of Europe, where the towns are close together, and the land between is covered with farms," protested the superior of the convent. "That rule is not possible to enforce in the wilderness of the New World."

"Nevertheless, I shall abide by it when I am able."

"I must remind you once again, Padre," the Father Guardian went on, "that it is a journey of a little less than three hundred miles to Mexico City. Much of the way lies through swamp, vast plain, and mountain, as I have told you. I am afraid it is a foolhardy undertaking."

"Permission has been given by the Father Commissary General of the Indies, and by yourself, " Junípero pointed out.

"Yes, I know, but I felt that I should not be doing my duty if I did not speak again of the dangers. I had two

Franciscan missionaries as they came and went.

extra mules brought, in case you changed your minds,"
said the Father Guardian, pointing to two animals as yet
unchosen by the friars.

Junípero went up to one of them, and spoke in a low,
polite tone. "Brother Mule, as long as I am able to walk,
you and your brothers will not be burdened with this
miserable body."

"No, Your Reverence," Junípero said, turning to the
superior, "Fray Pedro and I have made up our minds.
We walk to Mexico City. We start at daybreak."

"Very well, then," replied the other. "I shall have some
food packed for you to take with you."

"We shall require no food, thank you," Junípero
stated. "Divine Providence will take care of our needs."

"But, Padre, exclaimed the Guardian, "you have no

35

idea of the wild unsettled country through which you must go. There are miles and miles where no human being lives."

"We go on the Lord's journey, and the Lord will provide for us," said Junípero with great firmness.

The Father Guardian lifted his hands to heaven, shook his head, and left the courtyard.

A mule boy, who had been listening wide-eyed to the conversation, said to his friend, seated beside him on the hard-swept earth, "The friar may be ͺa good and holy man, Pablo, but he is stubborn."

"Yes," agreed Pablo, "as stubborn as one of our mules."

That night Junípero went to the convent hospital to say "Good-bye" to Francisco Palou. Poor Francisco! Shortly after the solemn Mass of thanksgiving that had been said when the ship had finally arrived in Vera Cruz, he had fallen a victim to the unhealthy climate of that port. At the moment he felt only very weary, but a tropical fever was to seize him later, which would bring him close to death. Junípero hated to go without his friend, but so eager was he to begin his work with the Indians, that he felt he must go at once.

As the first faint pearly light flecked the East the next morning, Padre Serra passed through the tall gateway to begin the first mile of thousands he was to cover on foot, as he brought Spanish civilization and the Christian religion to the Indians. With his brave companion, Fray Pedro, his prayer book and crucifix, he set out upon the high road with a song of praise in his heart.

The high road soon became a rough trail, though, that led through vast swamps. The evil-smelling marshes stretched on both sides, and in the broiling sun, the odor was unpleasant. When evening came, clouds of mosquitoes and other insects rose from the marshes and bit the missionaries until their skin was raw.

The exotic beauty of tropical vegetation brought a spirits-lifting response as the travelers made their way through stands of banana, palm, and mango trees, to broad plains that lay beyond.

Lush growth and wide plains finally were left behind, and they began to climb, as the rocky trail led through hilly country. They had to rest more often now, to save their breath. One time, darkness came upon them before they had reached the town where they were to find shelter for the night. A river, whose waters were dangerously high, lay between them and the town. They walked along the bank, but were unable to find a place shallow enough to cross. Their plight seemed desperate, especially as a storm was gathering.

"Let us ask Our Lady for help," said Fray Pedro, and Padre Junípero at once began the prayer.

When it was finished, they thought they saw something moving on the opposite bank.

"Is that a Christian on the other side of the river?" one of them called.

"Yes. What do you want?"

"We wish to cross the river, but cannot find a place to do so," they answered.

"Go along the shore until I tell you to stop," came the voice.

"Very well," they answered, and moved on.

They had gone quite a little way when the voice again came to them, "It is possible to pass at this point."

Removing their sandals, and lifting their robes, they were able to cross quite easily. On the farther bank, a well-dressed Spaniard greeted them in a friendly way, and invited them to his house for supper and to spend the night.

As they walked to his house, which proved to be some distance away, Junípero said, "I am curious to know, my friend, how you happened to be so far from home on such a dark, threatening night."

His only reply was, "I had gone on business."

This puzzled the friars, but as the man did not seem to wish to speak of it further, they were silent. Their wonder grew, though, when, in the morning, they saw that the rain which had fallen during the night's storm, had turned to ice. They knew then that they had been saved from freezing in that bitter night by the kind stranger.

At other times, too, help came to them in unexpected ways when their plight was serious.

After leaving the mountainous country, they passed through a valley where the sun seemed scorching after the coolness of the heights. The hardships of their journey were beginning to have their effect now, so that the friars grew very, very weary with each day's travel. Once, when they felt too tired to go farther, a man on horseback came along.

"Good day, Your Reverences," he greeted them. "You must be very tired. I hope you expect to take shelter soon. Where are you going to spend the night?"

"We expect to stay at that hacienda in the distance— if we can reach it," answered Junípero.

"Oh yes, you will find a welcome there. In the meantime, here is a pomegranate for each of you," the horseman went on, handing the fruit to them. "I think they will refresh you."

The crisp coolness of the little fruits not only took away their thirst, but their weariness, as well. When they reached the hacienda, they seemed not to feel tired, at all.

Another time an innkeeper, who had been their host for the night, gave them a loaf of bread as they set out in the morning. "It may be late before you reach the next inn," he said to them. "Take this loaf to eat along the way."

Thanking him, the pilgrims set out, but had not gone far when they met a beggar along the road. "Alms, alms, good padres," he pleaded. "I have not eaten for two days."

Since they could not turn the beggar away empty-handed, they gave him the bread.

They had still a long way to go before they should reach their night's shelter. As they had had no food to sustain them, they became more tired than usual. They found that they could not go on without resting for awhile. As they were seated by the side of the road, a man asked where they intended to spend the night.

On hearing their destination, he said, "You have quite a distance yet to go, Your Reverences, and you look tired. I happen to have some bread with me. Here, take it. It will give you strength to continue your journey."

So saying, he drew out a loaf, broke it in two, and gave one half to each. The friars expressed their gratitude, but when they looked at the bread, they were afraid to eat it.

"It is only corn mixed with water, and not properly mixed, either," remarked Fray Junípero.

"It seems to be only half baked," his companion added, and I am afraid it might do us harm to eat it."

Still, they were so weary and hungry that they decided to try it. Fray Pedro broke off a small piece to taste. "Why, Fray Junípero," he said in surprise, "it is really quite good, and seems to have been thoroughly baked."

Fray Junípero then tasted a corner of his loaf. "You are right," he agreed. "The flavor is excellent. It tastes as if it had been kneaded with cheese."

The bread not only tasted good, but even the small amount that they had to eat gave them renewed strength, so that they were able to reach their place of shelter by nightfall.

Thus it was that in time of need, unlooked-for help came

to them. Junípero Serra believed with all his heart that Divine Providence, Who knew their needs, had taken these means to supply them.

Not long before the end of their journey, though, misfortune stepped in to prove that the decision to make the trip on foot had, perhaps, been a foolish one. Covering many miles of rough, rocky roads each day in their heavy sandals, both friars suffered from bruised and swollen feet. Especially was this true of Junípero. At length, the condition of his feet was so grave that he was barely able to reach the night's shelter at an inn. That night he must have scratched the foot in his sleep, for the next morning a serious infection had begun. This was the source of a sore which spread up his leg, and never healed. It caused him to be lame and to suffer greatly for the rest of his life.

In spite of the condition of his foot, Junípero set out again after his one day of rest at the inn.

Limping and weary, he finally arrived, with Fray Pedro, at the shrine of Our Lady of Guadalupe, a few miles from Mexico City. It was the last day of the year 1749. Early on the first morning of the mid-century year he said Mass, and walked into the capital to the Franciscan College of San Fernando.

VI
The
First
Mission

Word of Junípero's fame as a pious friar, a scholar and preacher had traveled before him to the New World. At the College of San Fernando, the Father Guardian welcomed him warmly. Then an old friar threw an arm about his shoulders, and repeated the words that Saint Francis had spoken to the first Fray Junípero: "Would that some one might bring us a whole grove of junipers such as this one."

In sincere modesty Junípero answered, "It was not of my sort that Saint Francis spoke, but of a very different kind."

Padre Serra paid little attention to the glittering city which lay about the college walls. For two hundred years, ever since the conquest of Mexico by Cortez, the treasure which the Spaniards found there had been pouring into Mexico City. It was the largest and richest city on the

41

North American continent. Its buildings, such as the great cathedral and the palace of the governor, were magnificent. Many of the people who had come from Spain were very rich, and lived lives of ease and luxury. The city itself was on an island, and around it ran a canal. On this waterway plied many small boats, taking their fragrant flowers and crisp fruits to market. On the bank of the canal was a broad *paseo*, or avenue, where the wealthy people of the city might be seen.

Each afternoon, after the siesta, the beautifully dressed ladies of the city were driven in their fine carriages along the paseo. Beside them, on fine horses, galloped the men in rich attire.

It was a splendid show, but it was put on by only a few of the many thousands who lived in Mexico City. Most of these were poor and miserable, living in tiny dirty huts, with not enough food to eat.

The picture of Mexico City that remained in Junípero's mind always was the one he saw soon after his arrival. With another friar, he was walking along the great paseo called the "Alameda" one afternoon, when the showy parade of carriages and prancing horses came by. As the hundreds of richly bedecked vehicles rolled past, he was speechless with awe at their grandeur. Finally, a little apart from the rest, came the most splendid sight of all. Two ladies, dressed in green and purple satin, and laden with sparkling jewels, leaned against cushions of cloth of gold, which lined their coach. The coach itself, drawn by four glossy horses, shone with carvings of silver and gold set with precious stones. The driver and coachman sat proudly erect in their yellow livery. Riding at one side of the coach was a handsomely dressed gentleman on a lively black steed. His saddle was almost entirely covered with ornaments of silver and gold, and his riding whip was inlaid with mother-of-pearl. Around the horseman's hat was a band of diamonds which caught every ray of the sun, and sent flashes of brilliance all about.

Blinded by the shining beams from the diamonds, Junípero looked away. His glance fell on the entrance to a dark, crooked alley across the wide street. There in the shadows, on the muddy, filthy earth huddled a woman holding a baby. A torn blanket was her only garment, while the child was but partly covered with a few rags. The mother held a hand open for the coins of passersby, but the little one was too weak to lift his thin arm from his tatters.

Junípero's heart went out to those who suffered within sight of riches, but he had come to this new land for a special purpose, and he knew that he must get on with it. Shutting out the life of the great city, he turned his mind to the training for missionary life, which was to last for a year.

There were courses in teaching the Indians how to do the many kinds of work needed to carry on a successful mission. There were courses in the laws affecting the missions. There were even classes which taught the language courses spoken by some of the Indian tribes. Junípero found the language courses the hardest he had ever taken. It was always difficult for him to speak in a language other than his native Majorcan, or Spanish.

The months, filled with the preparations for the new life, went by peacefully. One evening in late May, Junípero and several of the other friars were strolling along the quiet paths of the garden of San Fernando, when they were joined by the Father Guardian.

"You cannot know how much satisfaction your arrival here has given me," the head of the college said to the missionaries. "Six years ago we started five missions in the Sierra Gorda region, but we have not been able to staff them with our own friars. In fact, we have often been forced to beg for mission workers from other colleges."

"Why is this so, Your Reverence?" asked one of the friars from Spain.

The Father Guardian was silent for a moment. Then he began slowly to tell the story of Sierra Gorda. "The Pamé Indians, who live in the wild rocky Sierra Gorda Mountains, were once very warlike. It was hard to subdue their fighting spirit, but finally, one of our finest military leaders brought them under control. But even though the Indians there have stopped their raids on the Spanish, and are largely friendly, it is difficult to keep our missions supplied with workers. The climate, being hot and damp, is unhealthy. The missionaries nearly always become ill after a short stay. We have found it necessary to recall them every six months, and send others out. This is not good because they do not stay long enough to learn the language. Then, too, supplies must be sent regularly, for the missions cannot grow enough food for their own support."

The Father Guardian sighed. Then he looked at the little group listening in the shadows. "I hope, now that you have come to work with us, that we shall no longer have to beg for missionaries from other colleges. Perhaps some of you will feel the call to go and work in the missions among the pagans of the Sierra Gorda."

Padre Serra's eyes shone in the deepening twilight. Here was the chance he had been waiting for! Moving to the front of the group, he said, "Here am I. Send me."

"And me, also," put in another.

"Send me, too," came from several more.

One of the voices which offered to go was that of Francisco Palou. Having recovered from his severe fever in Vera Cruz, he had come to San Fernando some time earlier.

44

With joy the Father Guardian accepted their offers, telling them to be ready to go in a short time.

So it was that Junípero was ordered to the Sierra Gorda, even though he had not finished his year's training. He was overjoyed to know that Francisco Palou was to go with him.

One morning in early June they set out for the Mission of Jalpán. With them was an escort of Mexican Indians and a soldier. There were several pack-mules and two saddle horses, also, but Junípero insisted on walking every mile to his first mission. The road was hard and rough, and before long his foot began to swell. The sore became very painful, but he paid little attention to it. To the end, he refused to ride the horse which trotted along beside him with an empty saddle.

At length, the Mexican Indians told the friars that they were approaching Jalpán. Climbing a ridge in the mountains, they saw among the crags in the distance before them, a group of small thatch-roofed wooden houses. This, the Indians said, was the mission. Despite the pain in his foot, Junípero hastened his steps.

Soon a lone Indian appearing from nowhere, approached them on the road. At the sight of the solitary figure, Junípero's heart bounded with joy. Here was the first of "his" Indians—the "brown brothers" for whose welfare he had come so far, and to whom he had pledged the rest of his life. Lifting his hand in blessing, he said in his kind, gentle voice, "*Amar a Dios* (Love God), my son."

The Indian only stared at him, not understanding, but the words were to ring out many years later, as Junípero and his Franciscans trod the dusty mission trails of California.

Though he was limping badly, Junípero almost ran the last yards of the way, so eager was he to arrive at his mission. Only when he stood in front of the wooden cross at the entrance, did he stop. There, clustered around the thatched wooden chapel, as well as closely packed about the smaller huts, were the mission Indians—nearly a thousand brown-skinned men, women, and children. Tears welled to the Padre's eyes as he blessed them. His heart was overflowing. At last he could actually begin the work for which he had given up all else.

According to the rules already in effect at the mission, the people were to gather in the church at sunrise for prayers and lessons in religion. On the first morning the church was filled, but as time went on, there was only a handful of Indians there. The others had gone hunting, fishing in the streams, or gathering roots and berries for food.

This state of affairs bothered Junípero very greatly. After a week or so he spoke of it to Francisco Palou. "One thing about our Indians is clear to me, Fray Francisco. We cannot hope to make good Christians of them unless we feed them. They must stay here at the mission, and receive daily training. As long as they need to go out to look for food, I fear we shall have little success in teaching them our holy religion."

"But how can we hope to feed so many?" Francisco asked.

"I intend to send at once for more supplies, so that we can assure all those who will come to stay in the mission that they will have enough to eat. I also shall send for seed corn and beans, so that we can start at once to plant crops which will provide food for all. Besides, we must have oxen and burros to help with the work, as well as cattle and goats. We ourselves must teach the Indians how to plant and grow their own food."

"You may always count on my help in whatever you undertake for the good of the heathens," Francisco assured him.

It was not long before the two friars could be seen in the mission fields showing their "brown brothers" how to plow the soil, plant the seeds, and care for the growing crops. On their heads were wide-brimmed felt hats to protect them from the blazing sun. Their heavy robes made such work in the damp heat very uncomfortable, but the brave missionaries never complained.

A few of the men learned the lessons in farming quickly. They were soon put in charge of the work, showing the others, under the friars' watchful eyes, how it was done.

The soil was poor, and water for the plants had to be brought a long way. The padres kept the Indians at their tasks, however, until all could see that their first harvest would be a good one.

Some of the women tended the crops, also, but most of them chose to make cloth on the looms that the friars had set up for them. They loved to see the slender threads being woven with their own hands into pieces of cloth big enough to make clothes for themselves and their families.

Padre Junípero directed the work of every minute of each long day, but he did not stop when the day was done. The candle in his tiny room burned far into the night.

Francisco, concerned about his friend's health, said to him one morning, "Your light was burning much too late last night, Fray, and for many nights. Your eyes show the lack of sleep. Anyone who works as hard as you do, needs his rest."

"I need something much more than rest," Junípero told him.

"And what is that?"

"I need to learn the language of our people. We can never hope to make the truths of our religion real to them unless we can speak in their own tongue."

"But Juan, our Mexican Indian, is very clever at teaching the language. Even I have learned a few words and phrases. He is with you all during the day. Must you study at night, too?"

"Just being able to speak to the people in the Pamé tongue is not enough. They must be able to pray in their own dialect, for prayer is a personal thing, and unless a person can speak to God in the childhood tongue that is a part of him, he cannot have a true bond with the Heavenly Father."

Francisco nodded. "Yes, of course you are right, Fray Junípero. And so you are trying to translate the prayers into Pamé? Is that it?" he asked.

"I have started with the 'Our Father'. It is very difficult, though, to find words in the Indian tongue to express the ideas of that great prayer. Besides," sighed Junípero, "you know how poor I am at languages." He was silent a moment, and then added firmly, "I am determined, though, to put the principal prayers, as well as the Catechism into the Pamé dialect."

Francisco knew that if Junípero Serra had determined to do a thing, it would be done. He said no more, therefore, about the candle burning at night, for he knew it would be useless.

As a result of untold hours of study, Junípero was, after some time, teaching the Indian children their prayers in their own language, as well as in Spanish.

It was a long time, though, before he could speak Pamé well enough to instruct his people in all the mysteries of the faith. Meanwhile, both he and Francisco felt that something was needed to help the Indians know more about the life of the Redeemer and His Blessed Mother.

"They are so simple and childlike," Francisco used to say, "that they cannot understand or imagine anything

48

they do not see."

"Then we must help them to see the great events in Christ's life," Junípero decided after he had been at Jalpán several months. "They love to act and to watch acting. Why shouldn't we, with their help, enact the great scenes of the Master's life?"

"The Christmas season will soon be here," suggested Francisco. "Might we not start with a Nativity play?"

"That is the very thing," agreed Junípero. "We shall build a stable, and have the scene of the Christ Child's birth."

"Like the one that our father, Saint Francis, made in his native Italy so long ago," mused Francisco.

"Yes, Fray Francisco. We must start at once to prepare our play." So eager was the padre that he limped out then and there to look for Juan, who would explain the plan to the people. "Juan! Juan! Come at once. I have work for you."

At daybreak on Christmas Day the church bells called the mission Indians and those in the nearby town to Mass. After the service was over, an Indian mother carefully laid her brown baby in the manger that had been built at the side of the altar. Then, in a robe the color of the sky, a little girl took her place at the baby's side, as the Blessed Mother. On the other side stood a young Saint Joseph. A gentle sheep, a burro, and a cow were led in, and stood gazing at the baby's face. The two children told the age-old story, then, in Pamé and in Spanish, while the people left their seats, and crowded about the scene.

One look at the faces of his people told Junípero that the plan had worked. Here was something lifelike. This they could understand. The birth of the One who came on earth to be their Savior would ever after be real to them.

49

At the other seasons of the year, when the Church celebrates the high points in the life of Christ, suitable scenes were enacted, too.

At the beginning of Lent a Chapel of Calvary was built on a hill outside the town. Every Friday Padre Serra, carrying a wooden cross so heavy that Francisco Palou could hardly lift it, led a procession of the Way of the Cross. Each time he put the sacred burden on his shoulders, he shut his eyes for a moment, and asked God for strength, just as he had done so long before when he had first carried the cross along the streets of Petra.

On Holy Thursday Junípero washed the feet of twelve of the oldest Indians, and ate with them. This was to make the sermon of Christ's humbleness at the washing of the feet, real to them.

On Good Friday he made the descent from the cross very lifelike by using a hinged figure of Christ which he had made. The figure, which had been placed on the cross, was tenderly taken down and put in a casket, while a procession was made to the lonely Lady of Solitude, the Blessed Mother.

The joy of Easter was felt by all the Indians when they saw the image of Mary carried out to meet the risen Savior.

These little plays and pageants moved the hearts of the once-warlike Pamés, as Padre Serra had hoped. Their love for the Son of God became so great that more and more of them moved to the mission to walk in the way of life He had pointed out.

VII
Mexico

Nine years had passed since the first Christmas at Santiago de Jalpán. The little girl who had stood beside the manger in the blue robes of the Virgin Mother now watched her own fat brown baby in his cradle. The boy who had told the Nativity story with her had become, like the real Saint Joseph, a builder. For several years he, with many of the Indian men, had worked on the new church of stone, which replaced the old wooden one.

The fields, with their neat rows of corn, peppers, beans, and pumpkins stretched beyond the mission buildings in all directions. Each family willing to plant and care for its own crops had been provided with a strip of land.

The prayers and Catechism had long since been put into Pamé. So successful had Padre Serra been in his religious teaching, that every Indian in the nearby town and the surrounding country had been baptized. Holy

Week had come to be a time of the most special devotion among these people. All the Spaniards who lived anywhere near knew of their pious celebration of this sacred time, and would move to the mission for the week in order to take part in the services.

In nine years, Fray Junípero, with the help of the faithful Francisco Palou, had made of Santiago de Jalpán a garden spot in the midst of the wild, craggy mountains of the Sierra Gorda; he had caused truly Christian hearts to beat in several thousand pagan breasts.

Then came the call from the College of San Fernando to leave Jalpán, and take over the missions on the Saba River. It was hard to leave the place where he had first brought the ways of a civilized life to the former savages. It was hard, too, to leave his brown children, to whom he had taught so well the lessons of the Christian faith.

Still, he was happy to have been called upon to try to change the warlike habits of the fierce Apaches who lived in the San Saba region.

He had been told very fully of the dangers involved, for two missionaries and a soldier had just been killed by the Indians there. Perhaps, thought Junípero, my dream of a martyr's death is going to come true, after all. On his last night at Jalpán, Junípero knelt in the church his own hands had helped to build. Here he renewed his promise to accept gladly the death of a martyr, if it came to him.

So, saying "Good-bye" to Francisco and the "brown brothers," and to all that he had accomplished in nine years, Padre Serra went to San Fernando to receive orders for his new assignment.

These orders were never to be given, though. By the time he had arrived in Mexico City, a military force had been sent out to punish the Apaches. Then a new Viceroy took office, and gave up the idea of making Christians of these Indians.

Instead of being sent back to Jalpán to his Pamé people, Junípero was kept in Mexico City. There he preached in the city itself for half of each year, and went out into the country for the other half.

The picture of the great city that he held in his mind became a reality again. It was largely the rich and powerful to whom he was preaching now. Most of them were religious people, giving freely of their money to the poor, and attending church regularly, but Junípero was not in sympathy with the easy, idle lives they led.

Still, he was pleased when he was asked to preach for the first time in the cathedral, for he knew it meant he was successful. He hoped, too, that he might be able to help his hearers lead better lives.

The magnificent cathedral was filled with people, for the name of Padre Serra was already known in the city. The great golden statue of Our Lady held up by four golden angels was like a patch of sunlight, throwing its rays over the people in front of the vast altar. In the rear of the church, another statue of Mary spread beams of moonlight from its pure silver form.

Junípero felt very humble in the spell of this beauty as he prepared to give his sermon, the first of a series, about which the cathedral congregation were very enthusiastic.

However, the longer he stayed in Mexico City, the more he felt that many of its people were very sinful. A sin is an injury done to God, he told them, and like any other injury it must be paid for. In order to make this need for payment, or penance, real to his listeners, he would strike his chest again and again with a heavy stone. In his right hand, he held aloft the cross, calling the people to repent.

In other ways, too, he inflicted pain on himself to show the people that they should pay for their wrongs by suffering.

Strangely enough, the citizens of Mexico City, for all their love of ease and luxury, responded to this kind of preaching, and Junípero Serra became one of the most admired men there, as he had been in Palma years before.

Here, again, though, his soul was not satisfied. When he rose in the pulpit, and looked at the pleasure-loving faces before him he longed for the plain, trusting, brown ones of his childlike Indians. It was to lead their simple souls to God that he had come to New Spain, he told himself, and not to preach to wise and worldly Spaniards. Then, with a rush of remorse, he would remind himself of the vows of obedience he had taken when he became a Franciscan. As long as he was told to stay in Mexico City he must do so gladly, without a word of complaint.

If his work in the city were not the sort he wished for, though, his journeys into the countryside of Mexico were more to his liking. To be sure, his travels brought many hardships, but he had always welcomed hardships if they were the means of bringing souls to God.

One of his journeys was to a city far to the south, where the bishop had invited him to come to conduct services throughout Lent. He and five other missionaries walked almost three hundred miles. Then, with Indian guides, they took canoes up the River Miges, which winds lazily through the jungle.

The sun beat down on their open boats with blistering heat. They longed to take shelter from its fierce rays on the river banks, where the tall trees and thick underbrush gave cool shade. The guides pointed to a great dark loop hanging from a tree limb near the shore, then another and another. They told the fathers that these were snakes whose bite was deadly. The canoes continued up the river.

As evening was coming on, the friars wanted to stop to camp for the night. Their guides seemed not to be in favor of this, but at last the canoes were beached near a spot where several small streams ran into the river. Before anyone had stepped ashore, a terrifying roar was heard, as a large dark-spotted yellow animal dashed from one of the streams into the thicket. Almost at the same moment, a gray streak with a black-tipped tail leaped from a tree on some tiny animal below. Without a word, the Indians started rowing, and did not stop that night, nor the next.

At length, they could see ahead of them a clearing in the jungle, where the river widened to a quiet pool. Perhaps here, the friars thought, they could go ashore, and straighten their numbed arms and legs. The waters seemed to be still, and the shore clear. When the guides were told to stop, they pointed their oars at long, brown, rounded objects near the banks.

"Are they logs?" asked one of the missionaries. His question needed no answer, for at that moment one of the "logs" moved, and the huge jaws of an alligator opened, while the friars looked on in horror.

For eight days and nights the journey continued. For eight days and nights the travelers could not get out of the canoes because of the dangerous life of the jungle. When they finally arrived at their destination, the men were almost paralyzed from the cramped position in which they had been forced to remain for more than a week.

On another occasion, Junípero was saying Mass at one of the churches far from the city. Just after drinking the Communion wine, he became so ill that he had to be helped from the altar, and could not go on with the Mass. For awhile it looked as if he would die of the poison that someone had put into the wine, especially when he refused to take an antidote brought by one of the Spaniards of the place. He could not, he said, take anything into his body so soon after the sacred wine of the Sacrament. Somewhat later, though, after sipping a little oil, the sickness passed, and he escaped death.

If the dangers and hardships were many, there were, too, some unusual rewards. One time Fray Junípero and another missionary had been conducting services for some weeks in a number of towns in a distant province. They were returning to Mexico City on foot when darkness found them far from an inn or place to spend the night. All about were cactuses and thornbushes.

"There is nothing to do but lie down in the open field," said Junípero.

"Let us go a bit farther on, though," suggested his companion. "We may find a better spot."

As they came around a bend in the road, they saw a small adobe house not far away, under three cottonwood trees.

"May there be a good Christian family living there who will give us shelter," said Junípero to the other, as they turned up the path to the house.

A kind-looking, rather elderly man greeted them. "Your Reverences are very welcome to our humble home," he said, opening the door wide.

In the room was a sweet-faced, smiling woman dressed in blue. By her side, sitting on the floor, was a quiet, mysterious child playing with a baby lamb. The supper they offered the friars was simple, but it was served with courtesy and hospitality. Before he went to bed that night, Fray Junípero raised his hand in blessing over the boy, who looked silently at him, and made the sign of the cross.

The next morning, after they had thanked the little

family, the priests went on their way. Soon they met some men driving mules. The muleteers stopped to speak to them. "Good day, Your Reverences," said one. "This is a lonely stretch of country. Where did you find a place to spend the night?"

"In a small adobe house by the side of the road," answered Junípero.

"House? What house?" asked the astonished men together. "In all the road you went over yesterday there is no house nor ranch."

"But we spent the night in it with the kind-hearted little family who live there," the friars assured the men.

"It cannot be," the stubborn muleteers insisted. "There is no house."

The two missionaries looked at each other, puzzled. Then Junípero fell on his knees. "Let us praise God for His watchful care, Fray," he said amid happy tears, "for, if I am not greatly mistaken, we have been guests of the Holy Family of Nazareth."

For seven years the country roads of Mexico felt the limping step of Padre Serra, and the churches of the great city echoed to his ringing voice. At length, while he was away from San Fernando on one of his journeys, the word came which meant his release from preaching, and the real beginning of his greatest missionary work. As soon as the letter from his college reached him, Junípero left for the city.

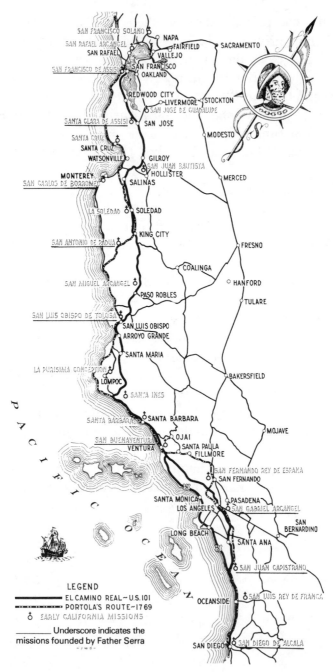

SAN FRANCISCO SOLANO
SAN RAFAEL ARCANGEL
SAN RAFAEL
NAPA
FAIRFIELD
VALLEJO
SACRAMENTO
SAN FRANCISCO DE ASSISI
SAN FRANCISCO
OAKLAND
REDWOOD CITY
LIVERMORE STOCKTON
SAN JOSE DE GUADALUPE
SANTA CLARA DE ASSISI
SAN JOSE
MODESTO
SANTA CRUZ
SANTA CRUZ
WATSONVILLE
GILROY
SAN JUAN BAUTISTA
HOLLISTER
MONTEREY
SAN CARLOS DE BORROMEO
SALINAS
MERCED
LA SOLEDAD
SOLEDAD
KING CITY
SAN ANTONIO DE PADUA
FRESNO
COALINGA
SAN MIGUEL ARCANGEL
HANFORD
PASO ROBLES
TULARE
SAN LUIS OBISPO DE TOLOSA
SAN LUIS OBISPO
ARROYO GRANDE
SANTA MARIA
LA PURISIMA CONCEPTION
BAKERSFIELD
LOMPOC
SANTA INES
SANTA BARBARA
SANTA BARBARA
MOJAVE
SAN BUENAVENTURA
OJAI
VENTURA
SANTA PAULA
FILLMORE
SAN FERNANDO REY DE ESPAÑA
SAN FERNANDO
SANTA MONICA
PASADENA
LOS ANGELES
SAN GABRIEL ARCANGEL
SAN BERNARDINO
LONG BEACH
SANTA ANA
SAN JUAN CAPISTRANO
SAN LUIS REY DE FRANCA
OCEANSIDE
SAN DIEGO
SAN DIEGO DE ALCALA

PACIFIC OCEAN

LEGEND
EL CAMINO REAL~U.S.101
PORTOLA'S ROUTE~1769
EARLY CALIFORNIA MISSIONS
_____ Underscore indicates the
missions founded by Father Serra
~ J W C ~

VIII
The
Story of
California

The Father Guardian met Junípero at the gateway to San Fernando. After raising his fingers in blessing, he said, "I sent for you, Padre, because an unexpected thing has happened. The King has ordered all the Jesuits out of New Spain. As you know, that religious order had many missions here."

"Yes, indeed, I know. They have done a fine work among the heathens," answered Junípero.

"Nevertheless, they have been ordered to leave the country, and we are to take over their missions. Do you know where Lower California is?"

"Only on the map. It has always seemed to me, as I have looked at maps of New Spain, that Mexico was a closed hand, with one finger extended, pointing to the other Spanish colonies of the New World."

The Father Guardian smiled. "Along that finger, the

Jesuits had sixteen missions. Our college has been asked to place friars in them. You know well our custom of allowing the members of our group to offer themselves for difficult missionary work. But in this case, since there was no time to ask you, I took the chance of saying you would go. I know how eager you always are to take on even the hardest appointment if it means saving souls."

"Because the missions will be without anyone in charge, except the military, after the Jesuits leave, it is necessary that you and our other Franciscans get there as soon as possible. Therefore, there will not be time for you to walk, as has been your custom on your missionary journeys."

Junípero nodded his head. "I understand the need for haste. Even our father, Saint Francis, would approve some other means of transportation in this case."

"His excellency, the Viceroy, has asked us to continue the policy of the Jesuits, at least until Don José de Gálvez arrives," the Father Guardian went on.

"I have only just heard of the new Inspector-General, Your Reverence. Do you expect him to go to Lower California himself?" Junípero asked in surprise.

"Yes. He has informed us that he will inspect the missions there in person. I may tell you, though, in confidence, that it is rumored he is planning to send an expedition to colonize Nueva (New) California—to the north."

California! It was years since Junípero had neard that magic word. At its sound, a tiny bell seemed to strike in his memory, and he remembered his far-off student days in Palma, when the name, "California," had summed up all the romance and wonder of the unknown New World.

There was not much time to think of the fabled land, though. In two days the missionaries were ready to leave for their new stations. Among them were his old friends, Francisco Palou and Juan Crespi.

The Father Guardian was in tears as he gave his blessing, for he felt that they were parting forever. "You go," he said, "with the blessings of God and our father, Saint Francis, to work in the mystic vineyard our King has given to our care. You are to have as your superior the good Padre Serra, whom by this patent I name as President of all the missions of Lower California."

Here his voice choked, and he handed the letter of patent to Junípero, who took it without being able to say a word because of his own tears.

Part of the journey was by land, and part by water across the Gulf of California. They finally arrived at Loreto in the "finger" of Lower California.

Loreto was a miserable little town of mud huts, but it was the capital of the province. Around it for miles stretched barren wastelands with only a few thornbushes and bare rocks to be seen here and there.

It was here at Loreto Mission that Padre Serra was to stay. Francisco Palou's mission, San Xavier, was the nearest to Loreto. From San Xavier, the missions reached to the south and north.

There was to be only one Franciscan at each, and Junípero's heart sank when he said "Good-bye" to the little group as they set out for their lonely stations. The old dread of loneliness clutched at his heart, not only for himself, but for his friends.

Like all the missions of the region, Loreto was in a very unhappy condition. After the Jesuits left, it had been turned over to a military commission. Most of the Indians, who were afraid of the soldiers, fled to the wilderness. Instead of attending to running mission affairs, the soldiers had spent their time vainly looking for the gold they thought the Jesuits had hidden.

Then, too, the Franciscans were to be in charge of religious teaching and services only. They had no clothing or food to give the Indians in order to appeal to them to come to the mission to live, and could not teach the people to grow their own food, or make their own clothing.

But Junípero was not discouraged. He decided to wait in his almost deserted mission until the arrival of the new Inspector-General. Perhaps, when he saw the state of affairs, some different rules would be made.

One afternoon Junípero sat in a high-backed leather-covered chair in the small study of his mission, with a large book on his knees. It was not often that he allowed himself the joy of reading. In fact, for many years he had been too busy for anything more than the Divine Office each day. Now, while he marked time at the quiet mission, he felt that he might take a few hours to delve into the small collection of books left by the Jesuits.

Ever since Padre Andrés, Guardian of San Fernando, had spoken the magic name, "California," the thought of it had lain at the back of his mind. If it were true that Don José de Gálvez intended to make an expedition to the north, Junípero felt that it would be interesting to know more than he already did about the history of that unexplored land. From the huge book before him, *The Conquest of New Spain*, he was piecing together the story of California.

The story of the real California, or "Upper California," as it was called, began in 1542 when Juan Cabrillo left the west coast of Mexico to look for the waterway which everyone thought must cross the continent from the Atlantic to the Pacific. The Spaniards called it the "Strait of Anián."

The "finger" of Lower California had been discovered earlier, in the days of Cortez, the conqueror of Mexico. At that time it was thought to be an island, and the first white man to reach it brought back stories about the many pearls to be found there. In fact, they called it the "Island of Pearls." This brought to mind an island in a romantic novel written by a Spaniard, Ordóñez de Montalvo, which was popular at the beginning of the sixteenth century. This book was about a strange island at the right hand of the Indies, where only women lived. It was ruled by a beautiful queen named Califra, and, according to the story, gold and jewels were everywhere. Weapons were made of gold, and so was the harness of the wild beasts the women of the island had tamed to ride.

Later, it was found that the "island" was really a peninsula, and a very dry and barren one. The name "California," though, came to be used for it, and the whole unexplored western coast to the north.

Cabrillo, with his two little ships, sailed northward against strong winds and currents. It took him three months to reach the harbor of San Diego. He and his men went ashore, where they were met by Indians, to whom they gave gifts of beads and trinkets. They went on up the coast, stopping at Catalina Island, San Pedro, and Santa Mónica, but failed to find any more good ports. Cabrillo died on the voyage.

For sixty years the Spanish forgot about California. In the meantime, Sir Francis Drake in 1578 had sailed his ship, *The Golden Hind*, into Drake's Bay, named the adjoining land "New Albion," and claimed it for his queen. Also, a Portuguese named Cermeño had been sent by the King of Spain to explore the western coast. He went ashore at Drake's Bay and San Luis Obispo. He made accurate soundings and wrote a good description of the shoreline.

Then the Viceroy of New Spain decided that the California coast must be explored for two reasons. The first was that the Manila galleon needed Spanish ports where she could take on food and water, and get warnings of pirates. This ship made the trip from the Philippine Islands to the west coast of New Spain each year with rich cargoes from the East. To get the best winds from the west, she had to sail far to the north, and come down the coast. The second reason had to do with the fear that England might try to start a colony in California on the basis of Drake's claim.

Therefore, in the year 1602 the Viceroy sent Sebastián Vicaíno with three ships, a map maker, and three Carmelite padres, as well as a good crew, to explore the coast of California. After landing at San Diego, they went up the coast until they came to a large bay, which they entered and named "Monterey" for the Viceroy. Of the bay Vizcaíno wrote: "We found ourselves to be in the best port that could be desired, for besides being sheltered from all the winds, it has many pines for masts and yards, and live oaks and white oaks, with water in great quantity, all near the shore."

The exploring party landed, and Vizcaíno set up a huge cross. At its foot the first Mass in California was said.

There the story of California ended.

Junípero sat in thought. Vizcaíno's discovery had taken place more than one hundred sixty years before. In all the time between, nothing had been done about the land to the north. And now - - - ?

The sun was setting over the neglected mission garden with a fiery glow, as the padre walked along the quiet paths. Suddenly a rider on horseback wheeled into the gateway, got down from his mount, and handed Junípero a letter. "From his excellency, Inspector-General José Gálvez," he said, bowing. Without waiting for an answer, the messenger got on his horse, and rode off.

"Don José is coming to look over the mission, I suppose," said Junípero to himself, as he opened the letter. But as his eyes traveled hastily over the pages, his hand began to shake, and a look of joy spread over his face. He sank down to read the message in the rosy beams from the heavenly bonfire.

The letter said that he, Gálvez, was planning to send an expedition into Upper California to start colonies at the ports of San Diego and Monterey. This was to be done with all haste, for word had come that the Russians had begun fur trading stations to the north, and it was feared that they might come on down the coast, and try to settle in California.

True to the promise made to the Pope soon after the discoveries of Columbus, when Spain was given the right to the western part of the New World, the King wished that the expedition be, first of all, a sacred one. It would have as its purpose the converting of the Indians to Christianity. The Franciscans had been chosen to start missions in Upper California, and he, Padre Serra, was invited to take charge of all the missions and missionaries. The letter went on to say that Gálvez thought it best to send two expeditions, one by sea, and one by land, to meet at San Diego.

When Junípero had read the letter over for the second time, he folded it, and sat with bent head. While the dying sunset grew pale in the west, his thoughts leaped on to the future, and strayed over the past. Here, at last, he thought, was the chance he had yearned for always— to be a pioneer of the cross. Now he could go into the wilderness home of the savages, and be the first to bring them the word of God.

Jalpán would always be dear to him because it had been his first mission. He had not started it, though.

He had only taken over and gone on with the work that had already been begun. At Loreto he had had so little chance to do anything, that he could hardly call it his own mission.

In California, though, he would have full charge, and there, please God, he would plant missions that would be oases in the pagan desert, where the simple natives would really be taught to lead Christian lives. San Diego would be the first, of course, and then Monterey. And after that - - - who knows?

The padre felt new life course through his being. He jumped up from his bench, and went in to send his reply to Gálvez. In it he said that the Inspector-General's plan was a good one. He said further, that he was ready to go in person with either the sea or land expedition, and that he would send as many other missionaries as were needed.

At sunrise a few days later he started for the nearby missions in order to tell the friars of the proposed plan. To the missionaries at a greater distance, he had written of it.

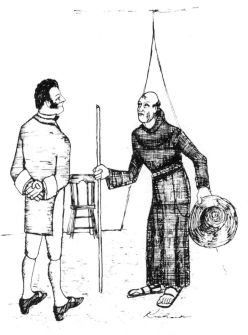

IX

Preparing
for the
Expedition

The fierce mid-morning sun beat down on a tent at Santa Ana, in Lower California, where the Inspector-General had made his camp. Don José de Gálvez rose from his chair as the tent flap was pulled back. Padre Serra stood in the opening, his broad-brimmed hat in one hand, and his tall wooden staff in the other. For a moment each looked at the other, measuring the manner of man he might be.

As his eyes grew used to the dimness of the tent room, Junípero was struck by the proud, stern face of the great man. In the thin line of the mouth there was determination relieved by a half smile. The quick, though unhurried steps he took toward the priest spoke of enormous energy. Here is a man who will carry out whatever he plans, thought Junípero.

For his part, Gálvez noted the bare, swollen feet in

their worn sandals, and the slender middle-aged body in its shabby, coarse, gray robe. The damp fringe of graying hair around the shaven crown topped a face to be remembered. The skin was tanned and leathery, the cheeks sunken from weariness. But in his eyes was a dream. Don José guessed that it was the dream of being Christ's pioneer in the unknown land of California. He knew that the friar had already walked nearly nine hundred miles in the last months to help the dream come true. Nothing but death itself would keep this amazing man from realizing it, finally.

Junípero came forward into the tent, and both men smiled.

"At last I have the honor to meet you, and discuss with you the plans for our expedition," said Gálvez. "Come, sit here. You must be tired after your long trip from Loreto. I shall have some chocolate brought in, and then we may look at this map of old Vizcaíno's explorations," and he pointed to a paper which covered a crude table nearby.

Later, as the two men sat facing each other across the table, Gálvez remarked, "We seek two shadowy harbors—San Diego, untouched for years, and the lost port of Monterey. Our expedition must go by little known seas and untraveled miles of wilderness where many savage tribes live. The hardships and dangers no one can foresee. Therefore, I think it wise to divide both the sea and land companies into two parts. At least one should get through."

"You divide your forces like Jacob in the Bible story," smiled Junípero. "An excellent idea, I think. There will be missionaries to go with each section, of course."

"That is what I wish," Gálvez said in turn. "Perhaps three with the expedition by water—one with each ship—and one with each land group."

"I will have them for you," promised Junípero.

"You, yourself, I think, should accompany the second land expedition with Portolá."

"You mean Governor Gaspar de Portolá?" inquired the friar.

"Yes. He is being sent as the Governor of California."

"Good!" commented Junípero. "He is an able man."

Gálvez glanced at the map. "There are to be forts at San Diego and Monterey," he told the priest. "I have sent for Lieutenant Pedro Fages and his Catalán Volunteers to go with you, as we have not a large enough military force here."

Padre Serra said nothing. Had he known how this man was to oppose him in the years to come in California, he might have spoken against him.

"I intend to order two packet boats, the *San Carlos* and *San Antonio* to sail for La Paz at once to carry the sea expeditions. Another ship will have to be brought here to carry enough supplies and equipment to start the missions," Gálvez told the padre.

Junípero searched the map again, his hand traveling over the routes that Gálvez had shown him. Long gray threads from his frayed sleeve made little designs on the paper. "And the missions?" he asked eagerly.

Gálvez smiled. Here was a man who drove straight to his goal. Nothing would cause him to swerve from his purpose.

"One at San Diego, near the fort. It will be called by the same name, since Diego was one of the saints of your order. Another near the port of Monterey—when it is found. It is to be 'San Carlos'. I have planned that as your mission, Padre. Between the two, at a spot which you shall select, a third one, named for San Buenaventura. May the good saint protect it always. Each of the missions will have its father, but San Buenaventura will

69

also have a foster father," Gálvez announced smilingly. "I like to think of it as 'my' mission."

"The government will supply the funds to equip the three missions?" asked Junípero.

"We must gather most of the church articles—vestments and the like—from the missions here in Lower California, I'm afraid," said Gálvez, frowning.

"But many of these missions are quite poor, and cannot spare the equipment," protested Junípero.

"Some money will be given us from the Pious Fund, to which many people in Mexico contribute," Gálvez told him. "All the missions here will have to donate religious articles, though. I dare not ask the government for too much, lest they think the expedition too costly, and give it up."

With that the padre had to be content.

As Junípero rose to go, Gálvez said, "I foresee this as a glorious chapter in the book of Franciscan missions, Your Reverence. I know that great credit will come from it to your order, and to its founder."

Junípero turned quickly to him. "And our founder—is there to be no mission named for our father, Saint Francis?"

"First, let him show us his harbor," said Gálvez with a laugh. "Then we will build him a mission there."

Up and down the "finger" of Lower California went Padre Serra, taking from each mission what it could spare for the infant missions to be started in the new land. "First of all, I must have bells," he said to himself. "We shall need those even before a church is built, to call the savages from the wilderness."

Ever since childhood, bells had spoken to his heart with many meanings. Now, these which were to call the natives from their life of savagery to one of Christian truth, would be special ones, indeed. There were some in

70

the mission belfries whose tones he liked particularly. Those he would take with him, he decided, and he began collecting them. When he had finished, there were seven large ones to be sent to the port of La Paz.

Besides the bells, there were baptismal fonts, silver cruets, censers, chalices, and many sets of brass candlesticks. Pictures there were, too, from some of the chapels, and images of the Virgin, Jesus, and Saint Joseph. There were nineteen sets of vestments for the priests to wear at Mass.

When he had ordered these things sent to La Paz, Junípero hastened there himself. What a busy place the port was, as everyone hurried to pack the supplies and equipment into boxes so that it would be ready when the ships arrived. As usual, Padre Serra did not spare himself where there was work to be done. Even the Inspector-General packed the sacred articles for "his" mission himself. When they were all carefully placed in boxes and made ready, he noticed that Junípero was still working at his, with bells and candlesticks piled up around him.

"Ha!" said Gálvez, jokingly, "I think I am a better sacristan than Your Reverence. All the things for San Buenaventura are packed."

"Then," answered Junípero, with a twinkle in his eyes, "you can help me finish mine."

Gálvez laughed, and went to work with a will.

When the *San Carlos* arrived, Gálvez went aboard, and inspected the ship carefully. She was leaking, and the Inspector-General decided that the ship should be repaired and recaulked.

"But, your honor," said the crew foreman, "there is no rosin for caulking it."

"Then we must find a substitute," said Gálvez without hesitation. "Bring several of your men, and come with me."

71

Leading them to a thicket outside the town, the great man began to show the men how to cut gashes in the trunks of the tree cactus. The sap that ran out, he caught in pails they had brought along. This served the purpose of rosin very well, and the repair work went forward.

A great deal of food was taken aboard for the explorers. There were sides of salted and dried beef, heaps of beans, and strings of red peppers. There were chains of garlic, barrels of flour, chocolate, and figs. Seeds, from both the Old and New Spain were taken along to be planted in the new land—vegetables, flax, and flowers.

Farming implements and the tools which would be needed about the new missions were put aboard, too.

The *San Carlos* was ready to sail on January 9, 1769. Early in the morning Padre Serra said Mass in honor of Saint Joseph, who was chosen as the patron of the expedition. Then he blessed the ship, the flags, and all sixty-two persons aboard. "Go now," he said, "with the blessing of Almighty God, and we shall all meet again at the port of San Diego, to which He will guide us."

As soon as the white sails had spread themselves in the breeze, and the *San Carlos* was under way, Junípero went back to Loreto to prepare for the land expedition. He stopped at Mission San Francisco Xavier to tell Francisco Palou of all that had happened.

X

The Beginning of the Journey

By the time Junípero left Loreto, the *San Antonio* had left La Paz, and the first land expedition had been on the road a month. The main part of the second company, under Governor Portolá, left Loreto before Easter, but Junípero decided that he must remain at his mission to perform the Easter services.

On March 28, he set out with the two soldiers and a servant whom the governor had left behind to accompany the friar. The sun was just peering over the eastern rim of the world as he started on his great adventure. He was fifty-six years old, very tired, and much more lame than usual. He took with him only a loaf of bread and a bit of cheese for his body's food, but his soul feasted on the thought of the great work he was about to begin.

As he limped into the mission of San Xavier at dusk

on the first day, Francisco Palou met him at the gate. Tears were in the old friend's eyes as he noted the swollen foot and the leg with its huge sore. "Fray Junípero," he said after he had greeted him and taken him inside where the lame padre could be seated, "you must be able to see for yourself that you cannot go on this long journey with your foot in its present condition. It will be far too painful for you, and may be the cause of holding back the expedition. Let me go in your place. Though my ability to convert the heathen does not match yours, my health and strength are greater. These are needed for such an undertaking. I pray you to remain, and let me take your place."

Junípero was silent for a moment. Then he said calmly, "Do not let us speak of this. I have unlimited confidence in God, whose goodness will allow me not only to arrive in San Diego to set up and dedicate in that port the standard of the holy cross, but also to go on to Monterey."

Francisco saw that it was useless to try to keep him from this journey. He had to content himself with giving his friend some extra food and clothing for his greater comfort, and to let him rest in his mission for the next three days.

There was much to talk about, for Fray Francisco was to become Father President of the Missions of Lower California when Padre Serra left. There was also something to write each day, for the traveler had decided to keep a diary of his trip. He felt that in time to come, this journey would be of interest to his Franciscan brothers. Each night, therefore, he would write in his small, neat letters the events that had taken place during the day.

As day was breaking, Junípero rose to start on his journey. He had agreed to ride the mule he had brought, but when he tried to mount it, two soldiers had to lift him bodily, and place him in the saddle.

He turned cheerfully to Francisco, though, and bade him good-bye: "Adiós till I see you in Monterey, where we shall come together to work in the vineyard of the Lord."

Francisco was so saddened by his old friend's helplessness that he could only say tearfully, "Adiós—until eternity."

"Why, Francisco, 'thou of little faith', your words of doubt have gone to my very heart." Such was the sad parting of the two who had left Majorca together so long ago to work in the heathen lands of the New World.

The little party of four journeyed on through the hot semi-desert of Lower California. There were no inns, so when they could not reach a mission by nightfall, they slept on the ground.

One evening, as they were setting up their camp, a miserable little group of Indians came up to them. The children were whimpering, and their elders told Junípero that they had been wandering for days, looking for food. They had once lived at a mission some distance away, but when the friars had not been allowed to supply them with food, they had left to look for their own. As soon as the padre heard this, he went to one of his pack mules, and took a bag of corn meal, which he gave them. "Take this," he said, "and after we have given thanks to God together, return to the mission, for food is on the way to you by sea. Our good Inspector-General has seen to it that the missions will once again be supplied."

They all gathered around the missionary, and said a few prayers. Then they began to sing a little song of God's love, which they had been taught at the mission. As the tender notes rose toward the bright stars of the southern sky, Junípero's heart soared with them, and he dedicated himself once again to helping these "brown brothers" in the unknown land which lay ahead.

At each mission along the way, the Father President stopped for a few days in order to break the loneliness of the solitary life of the friars. One of these missions was Santa Gertrudis, built on a rocky ledge in a narrow, dismal canyon, shut away from the rest of the world. Fray Dionisio, a brilliant young Franciscan, who had been with Junípero on his journey down the River Minges, was stationed there. The one soldier and servant who had been with him were taken by the Captain of the first land expedition to California as he had passed through.

"It is terrible, Your Reverence. There is not anyone with whom I can talk, for I know little of the Indian language, and there is no one in all the country around who knows one word of Spanish." A cloud passed over the young friar's face, and he shuddered deep within himself.

Junípero remembered a far-off time in Palma when to him, too, loneliness had seemed the one burden which a human being was not able to bear. Throwing an arm about the younger man's trembling shoulders, the Father President tried to console him.

"I shall write to the Inspector-General to ask if it is possible to send you at least one soldier," he replied, "but I am not at all sure that it can be done."

Fray Dionisio sat for a long time with his hands covering his face. When he took them away, the unhappy, hunted look in his eyes made the older man fear for his sanity. When the little band left the mission after five days, Padre Serra vowed that in the missions under his charge there would always be at least two friars, if that were at all possible.

At the Guadalupe Mission, the friar in charge had persuaded a fifteen-year-old Spanish speaking Indian boy who knew how to assist at Mass, to accompany the padre as interpreter.

Early in May, Junípero reached Santa María on the frontier, where Governor Portolá, with part of the expedition were camped. After some expected supplies arrived, they joined those of the party who were at Velicatá. This was a few miles away in a spot where there was good pasture for the animals.

As Junípero looked about him, and learned from the soldiers that there were many Indians living nearby, an idea came to him. He went with all haste to Portolá.

"Your Honor," he said, "it seems to me that this would be a good place for a mission. There is water and grass, and these little huts the party has already built could serve as a beginning. Moreover, it is nearly one hundred eighty miles to the next mission."

Portolá thought for a while. "It would serve to bridge the missions of Lower California with the ones we shall start in the new land, too," he observed. "I think your idea is a good one, Your Reverence. It must be done at once, though, for we cannot delay our departure for San Diego."

"Tomorrow is Pentecost. Let us dedicate it then, and leave here as the missionary, Padre de la Campa, who came with you."

A large cross and some bells were set up before one of the huts, where Mass was said. It was a strange service, with only the light of one candle, the sound of the soldiers' muskets for music, and the odor of the drifting smoke from their firing as incense.

Junípero looked in vain for even one Indian to come near as he founded his first mission, but the next day, as the expedition was ready to set off, word came to him that a group of natives was coming near. He happily went out to meet ten men and two boys. He was shocked to see that they wore no clothing. Putting both hands on the head of each, he blessed them. Then he filled their hands with dried figs. They, in turn, presented the friar with a net full of fish. He accepted the fish with thanks, though he knew they were spoiled. The Indians agreed to come to the mission when they were in need. Junípero was content, for he felt that they would soon be converted.

Leaving Padre de la Campa part of the cattle, some mules, and food, the party set out. The next day they came to San Juan de Dios, where Sergeant Ortega, with some of his soldiers and part of the beasts, were waiting.

At last all of the expedition were united, and Junípero, like the others, was eager to be on the way. But then, without warning, disaster struck. His foot and leg, which had given no trouble in the excitement of founding the mission at Velicatá, became so inflamed, swollen, and painful, that he could not walk, stand, or sit. He could only remain stretched upon his bed in the rude shelter the soldiers had built of tree boughs. There Governor Portolá came to him.

"Padre Serra," he said, "it distresses me greatly to see you in this condition. I had looked forward to our settling California together. Now, of course, it is clear that you cannot go on. If Your Reverence will permit, you can be carried back to Velicatá in order to recover there. The rest of us will go on our journey."

Though he was suffering an agony of pain, the brave man said in his quiet, determined way, "Please do not speak to me further about it, because I trust in God to give me strength to go to San Diego, as He has given it to me to come this far. In case it is not His wish for me, I shall resign myself to His Holy Will. Even if I die on the road, I will not go back. You can bury me here, and I

Friars receiving the Fr. Guardian's blessing before departing for California.

shall gladly remain among these heathen people if it is the Will of God."

Seeing that he could not change the priest's mind, the governor withdrew. Soon a servant came in and told Junípero that Portolá had ordered a litter made of small branches so that he could be carried by the Christian Indians who were in the party.

"Oh no, that will be too hard for the poor Indians," said Junípero. "I must not cause them this extra work."

For some time he lay with closed eyes, praying that in some way the pain might be lessened so that the Indians would be spared this burden. Late in the afternoon he sent for the servant. "Ask the mule boy, Juan Coronel, to come to me," he ordered.

"My son," he began when Juan appeared, "don't you know how to make a remedy for me?"

"But, Padre, I know nothing about remedies. I am not

Founding of Mission San Diego, July 16, 1769.

a doctor. I am only a muleteer, and I only know how to cure pack sores on the backs of mules."

"Then pretend that I am one of your mules, and that this is a pack sore. The pains are so great that I cannot sleep, so please make the remedy, and apply it just as if I were one of your pack animals."

Juan Coronel laughed, and said, "I will do it, Padre, to please you."

He went out of the hut and gathered some herbs that were growing there. He crushed them between two stones, and mixed them with some tallow. Then he heated the mixture well, and applied it to the foot and leg.

Soon Junípero began to feel drowsy, and before long he was sleeping peacefully. He did not waken until daybreak, and he was so much better that he arose and said Mass as if nothing were wrong.

XI
The Journey Goes On

The mules' bells jingled, the soldiers' muskets rattled, the cattle herders' long whips cracked in the soft morning air, and the long caravan got under way. Junípero, his face aglow with the joy of the beginning of this sacred trek, stood on a tiny knoll by the side of the path, and looked far ahead to the point where Sergeant Ortega was leading the way. With him were part of his soldiers in their leather jackets which would protect them against Indian arrows. A few of the mission Indians with spades, crowbars, and axes to cut away the brush, and open a passage where it was needed, were at the front also. Governor Portolá, on his fine, glossy mare, and the officers came riding by next. The mission Indians, and others who were walking, followed the riders. Behind them were the pack animals and the cattle, which numbered almost two hundred. The remainder of the soldiers

81

acted as a rear guard, bringing the great procession to an end. Like a long, living, noisy, moving rope it coiled along the trail left by Captain Rivera Moncada and the first expedition.

The travelers toiled over dry, bare wastelands where water holes were scarce, and often were, in fact, mud holes. Beasts and men suffered from thirst. They scrambled over rocky hillsides where the howl of the mountain lion was heard during the night hours, as they camped under the stars.

Then, a lone cottonwood tree, standing tall and leafy in the brown countryside, was the advance messenger of a different kind of land. Green grass covered the rolling hills, and tiny flower faces smiled up at the tall trees whose branches waved protectingly over them. A few rabbits scurried among the trees, and later there were deer and antelopes.

Junípero watched each day for the "brown brothers" whom he had come to teach. Often there were signs of small villages abandoned in haste as the Spaniards approached, but no Indians were seen during the early part of the trip. Once two dark forms appeared at the top of a hill, but they fled at once.

The next day two more were seen, and the mission Indians traveling in the party were sent to get them. The padre wished to tell them that the white men were their friends. Both were caught, but one slipped away. The other had to be tied and dragged into camp, kicking and straining at the ropes. His long hair, bound with a strand of blue wool, fell over his face. While he knelt, struggling, on the ground, Junípero gently put his hand on the young Indian's head, and recited the Gospel of Saint John. This frightened the poor savage more than ever, so the priest made the sign of the cross over him, untied him, and gave him some dried figs. Portolá and the others gave him meat and tortillas, also. He managed to eat a little of the food, and to tell them that his name was Axajui. He was still very frightened. Before leaving, however, he told them of a plot by the natives of several villages to hide behind some cliffs, and spring out to kill the Spaniards as they passed by. He was ordered to tell his people that the white men were their friends, and meant them no harm. Apparently the Indians believed him, for nothing came of the plot.

If the Indians fled before the coming of the caravan in the early part of the journey, they made up for it later, to the annoyance of all but Junípero. One time four of the savages were found lurking near the camp in the early morning as the pack animals were being loaded for the day's march. They were held for awhile inside a circle of soldiers as they heard Mass. It pleased Padre Serra to see them there, but the savages were anything but pleased. When they joined about forty more of their number who had approached the camp, there were angry shouts and threatening movements towards the Spaniards.

"José," said Junípero to his Mexican Indian boy, "what are they saying?"

"They say, 'Turn back, white men, turn back. Do not come farther into our country.' "

The natives refused to leave, even when four soldiers on horseback, riding close together, forced them to back up. Finally, two musket shots had to be fired in the air, which sent them off in a hurry.

This did not keep others from following the expedition in great numbers, however, later on. Junípero was joyful as he looked back at the end of the parade, and saw the "brown brothers" straggling along behind it. The soldiers were not so happy. They did not like the disposition of this tribe, and they kept on their leather jackets and shields, while they held their hands ever on their weapons. For now, the hills of the Contra Costa were closing in on them, and the men feared an ambush.

All went well, though, until they came upon a very different kind of tribe—extremely friendly and full of mischief and childish antics. The first of them, a group of twelve men, laughing merrily, approached the Spaniards one evening, and offered to show them a good place to camp for the night. When the tents were set up, and all was ready, Junípero sent his servant and José to them with some figs and meat.

"Tell them that they may come to us without fear," the padre told José, "and that we should be happy to have them come to greet us, for we are their friends."

José returned, saying that they seemed friendly, and would come later when they could bring some gifts which they had sent for from their village nearby.

As the sun was sinking in the west, they appeared with nets full of cooked fish which they gave to the travelers. All had their bows, arrows, and other weapons. They put these on the ground, and stepped back, all except two. One of the two then began to act out the way in which a weapon was used, and the other was the victim. The first would pretend to loose an arrow from the bow. The second would clap a hand over a spot on his arm, his face twisted as with pain. Then the first warrior would send another arrow flying. The other clutched his heart, staggered for a moment, and fell to the earth, still. Two more would take the stage then, and show how another weapon was used.

As the Spaniards were enjoying this playacting, two Indian women appeared, talking rapidly. Unlike the men, who had no clothing at all, the women wore a skin apron front and back, hanging from a thong about the waist. They also had a long cape around their shoulders. The younger woman, the wife of the village chief, carried on her head a large doughy pancake she was bringing as a part of the Indian gift to the white men.

Padre Junípero rose at once from his seat on the ground, and walked forward. "You are welcome to our camp, my daughters," he said.

Not noticing the pancake, he raised his eyes to heaven, and placed his hands on the young woman's head to bless her. Much to his surprise, his hands sank into the soft dough. When he lifted his fingers, they were covered with the white sticky mixture. He was extremely embarrassed, especially when the chief stepped up and joined his wife in explaining the proper way of eating the pancake. The older woman also added some comments in a loud harsh voice.

The next morning, as the expedition was setting out, the Indians appeared, to escort the travelers on their way, which was along narrow paths at the edge of steep cliffs. Their love of mischief almost brought ruin to the party. Like unruly children, they climbed to the tops of the slopes above the trail, and slid down, laughing and yelling in glee. This frightened the horses and pack mules so that they jumped and bolted in all directions, with the muleteers scurrying after them. This only added to the fun for the merry Indians. Each time the beasts would plunge and rear, the savages would shriek with delight, and scramble up the hill to tumble down in front of them again. Before long, there was near panic in the line of march. When it was seen that the animals were in danger of falling over a cliff, Portolá called the chief, and asked him to put a stop to the game. The people would not listen to him, though, and finally the Governor ordered that a musket be shot in the air. In surprise and fear, the mischievous savages fled, not to return.

"That has ended our trouble," Junípero said to Portolá, "but I feel that they left us with some doubt of our love toward them."

This saddened the friar, for he hated to leave the *Gentiles*, as the Spaniards called the natives, at all, without being able to bring them to God and the ways of civilization. As often as he could, he would say to them the words, "Jesús, María," hoping that they might keep the holy names in their hearts.

One evening, a group appeared shortly after the evening meal. Junípero seated them about the campfire. When he had blessed them all, a young mother put her baby in his arms. As he held the child, gently patting its brown arms and legs, the padre kept repeating, "Jesús, María." Solemnly, their eyes shining in the firelight, their heads bobbing up and down with the effort, the Indians said the strange words over and over.

"All the 'Gentiles' have pleased me, but these, especially, have stolen my heart from me," he wrote in his diary.

Dancing was a particular delight of theirs. Specially trained dancers went about carrying rattles, gourds, and decorated sticks for their performances.

The happy, carefree, wild lives of these people seemed to have an overpowering appeal for the mission Indians who were with the Spaniards. They began to desert from the expedition, nine of them vanishing at once, without leaving a trace. Junípero was stunned and puzzled at their disappearance, but remembered them in his prayers, asking the Lord to bless them for the help they had given on the journey.

For some time the trail led through the lands of these gay, fun-loving tribes. They had no sense of wrong in trying to take anything they saw that pleased them. Strangely enough, for men who wore none at all, clothing appealed to them most of all. They tugged at the friar's robe, begging him to take it off, and give it to them. They even tried to take Portolá's boots and leather jacket. It was when Junípero's spectacles disappeared, though, that he almost, but not quite, lost patience with his beloved *Gentiles*.

A large group had gathered around him at the camping place. They were pressed tightly against him, clutching his robe, fingering his wooden rosary, examining his sandals. A woman at the rear of the crowd noticed his silver-rimmed eyeglasses. Here was something delightful, indeed! At once they all started pointing at them, and asking by motions, for him to take them off. Smiling, he obligingly removed the glasses, and held them up for all to see. Quick as a wink, they were snatched away. For a minute Junípero caught a glimpse of them shining in the sunlight as they passed from hand to hand. Then they were gone. In vain he pleaded for their return as the gathering broke up into little groups, and wandered off.

In dismay, the poor friar thought of his plight. He would be almost helpless without the aid of spectacles. It would be months, he knew, before others could be sent from Mexico. He was desperate as he went from group to group, begging the Indians to tell him where the glasses were. They merely looked at him, and shook their heads. Finally, he heard two women arguing in a loud voice. Limping quickly to the spot where they stood near some bushes, he saw that his precious spectacles were the cause of their argument. Junípero had some trouble getting them away from the two, who wanted them as a decoration. When he offered the women some beads in exchange, however, they finally gave up the glasses. With a sigh of relief, and a thankful prayer, he returned to camp.

He was especially thankful that the women had considered the beads a fair exchange. Sometimes the soldiers and muleteers had not been so lucky. They had been trading with the natives for some time because the party's food was becoming scarce. These coast people were good fishermen, and they were willing to trade their fish for cloth and trinkets. They were especially fond of the white handkerchiefs the Spaniards had brought with them. Soon they became very shrewd merchants, though, demanding one large handkerchief, or several small ones, for a large string of fish, while a smaller one was enough for a smaller catch. The men wondered what would happen when the handkerchiefs were all gone.

As the expedition neared Upper California, they came upon still another tribe of savages. Like their neighbors to the south, they loved fun, but there was a meanness and ill will mixed with their mischief. They were in a land where small streams ran between high banks of soft, slippery mud. It was hard for the animals and men to keep their footing. These Indians, all with bow and arrow, would dart in among the mules, frightening them. They would disappear, and then dash in among the animals again, shouting with laughter. When camp was made, they stayed with the travelers, imitating all their actions, and laughing at them.

The soldiers begged to be allowed to fire their muskets in the air to frighten them off, but Padre Serra and Governor Portolá shook their heads. "We are nearing the Indians whom we hope to convert," warned the padre. If they heard of such a frightening action, it would be a long time before they would trust us. We must try to have patience, and overlook the annoyance..."

One thing which helped them to endure the irritating antics of the savages was the increasing beauty of the land. Each day it grew lovelier. The fresh, green, leafy trees nudged the blue of the sky. Smiling, grassy meadows stretched from the trail to the rising slopes beyond. Sparkling streams of sweet cool water hurried noisily over their rocky beds.

Junípero's heart ached with delight at the sight of the wild flowers which the hand of the Great Artist had splashed with the most exquisite colors for the pleasure of His children. Huge patches of red, yellow, and blue dotted the green fields; small clumps of white and purple hugged the streams, where vines hung heavy with unripe grapes. Most beautiful of all to him was the wild rose, remembered from childhood. "Today," he wrote in his diary, "we have met the queen of them all, the rose of Castile. When I write this, I have before me a branch of rose bush with three roses opened, others in bud, and more than six unpetaled. Blessed be He who created them." He named the place where the first ones were found "Arroyo of the Roses."

The bright countryside made the traveling easy, but in the distance were rugged hills. When the party reached them, they found the slopes even steeper than they had feared. Partly walking and crawling, they scrambled up, only to fall back, and stumbled up again. When they reached the top, they found the other side to be so straight and sheer that they slid down most of the way, the earth seeming to slip away beneath them. At length the valley was reached, and they knew that their journey must be nearing its end.

They were sure of it when they saw two "Gentiles" dressed in blue tunics standing on a low ridge in the distance. The blue cloth could only have come from several bales of cotton of that color which the first land expedition had brought to clothe the natives. The good news brought by these Indians was that the party was only two days from San Diego, and that Sergeant Ortega and a soldier who had gone on ahead to find water and a camping place, were already at the port.

The next day ten soldiers from the first expedition appeared to escort the Governor and his companions to San Diego. Portolá, with several soldiers, went on at once. The rest followed with the tired pack animals.

There were still steep passes and rough, rocky hills to be climbed. Now, at last, the hardships of the journey began to tell on Junípero. He was so weary that he doubted if he could finish the trip. He pushed on, though, as usual, and his reward came when he reached the top of the last rocky hill, and shading his eyes with his hand looked at the view below.

There, on the calm, unruffled waters of the bay nestled among rolling hills, rode two ships with furled sails. In the soft, still air of that morning of July 1, 1769, it seemed to the almost exhausted friar as if he were gazing on a painted scene, far-off and lifeless. Then, slowly, he began to be aware of its meaning, and he was stirred to the depths of his being. Here before him lay this beautiful harbor on which no white man's eyes had rested for more than a century and a half. Here was the gateway to the fabled land of California. And through that gateway he, Junípero Serra, was about to enter, bringing the cross of Christ and the ways of Spanish civilization to the un-known hordes of pagans who lived within it. The weari-ness of the forty-six day journey from Velicatá fell from him. It was the beginning of a new day in his life of service to God—the day toward which all the others had been pointing. As the soldiers came up and fired their muskets, and received an answering salute from the ships' guns in the harbor, his overflowing heart saluted the new day.

XII San Diego

At the foot of a hill near the curving sands that edged
the blue Bay of San Diego was a stockade built of sap-
lings. It surrounded a few brushwood and tule huts, and
a corral. Forgetful of his weariness and his lame leg,
Junípero hurried to the open gateway, eager to see those
who had come by sea, and with the first land party.
What a meeting it would be! The four parts of the great
expedition planned by himself and Gálvez in the sun-
drenched tent at Santa Ana had come together at last
at the legendary port of San Diego.

The first to welcome him was his old friend, Fray Juan
Crespi and then the three other missionaries. The two
ship captains were on hand, as well as Captain Rivera y
Moncada, Sergeant Ortega, Doctor Pratt, and Portolá.
Junípero greeted them all warmly. Then he looked at the
few pale, thin soldiers and the remaining bedraggled

91

mission Indians who had gathered around. Suddenly he realized that something was wrong. "Where are the others?" he asked, looking from face to face, with misgiving.

Silently Fray Crespi pointed to rows of grave mounds on the beach, and then to the huts. "Dead and dying, or ill," he said sadly.

Junípero looked at him in unhappy surprise.

"Come into the hut, Padre," said Portolá, "and hear the sad story."

Juan Pérez, a countryman of Junípero and Juan Crespi, and captain of the *San Antonio* began: "It was the 11th of April when we dropped anchor in San Diego Bay. To our surprise, the *San Carlos* which, you will remember, Padre, had sailed more than a month before we did, was nowhere to be seen. Neither was there any sign that the land expedition was near.

"I should have liked to have gone north at once in search of Monterey. I could not do so, though, for Gálvez's orders were clear. Whichever ship arrived first was to wait twenty days for the other one.

"We saw Indians on the beach, but since we did not know if they were friendly, we thought it best not to go ashore. There were no soldiers, you will recall, aboard the *San Antonio*.

"For eighteen very dull days we rode at anchor. Then, at sundown, as we were getting ready to sail north when the twenty days were up, the *San Carlos* hove into sight. She cast anchor, but no gun salute answered ours, and no boat was lowered. I knew something was amiss, so I went over at once in one of the small boats. What a sorry sight met my eyes! Captain Villa and his entire crew had fallen victims of scurvy."

Junípero's eyes questioned Villa, who took up the tale: "Our plight was due to several things. We were much

92

delayed, first because we thought the port was farther north, and went far beyond it. Our food was almost gone, and the water entirely so. We went ashore for water, but it was impure. When the sickness struck my men, they were not strong enough to resist it. It is only by God's grace that we were able to make port. When we did, we could not lower a boat because there were too few men well enough to do it. Captain Pérez of the *San Antonio* did what he could for us, but for most of my crew it was too late."

The captain's voice was choked, and he was unable to go on. Padre Serra placed his hand on the other man's arm in sympathy. Then he turned back to Captain. Pérez. "You brought the poor souls ashore, Juan?"

"Yes, my men built tents on the sand out of sail cloth. We brought all the sick to the shelters, and tended them as best we could. Doctor Pratt, though sick himself, supervised the nursing with the help of the friars. But alas, my men from the *San Antonio* took the disease, too. Soon it was a matter of the sick caring for the dying, and any who were strong enough digging graves for the dead. Just when the end for all of us seemed in sight, Captain Rivera y Moncada arrived to save the day."

The leader of the first land party took up the story: "When we arrived six weeks ago, and saw two ships in the bay, we expected to be greeted joyously by all the sailors and others who had come by sea. Instead, only a few pale, sunken-eyed men staggered weakly out of the tents on the sand dunes to meet us. My men were all in good health, and we started at once to build this camp here on higher ground. The sick were carried to that part of the camp which we made a hospital," and he pointed to a section at a distance from the hut in which they sat, "while the rest of us stayed here. All who have kept their health, or recovered from the sickness, have worked day and night in nursing the sick."

Padre Serra looked at those about him, stunned. "And how many have we lost?" he asked finally.

In a hushed, sad voice Captain Villa of the *San Carlos* answered, "Only two of my crew—the cook and one sailor—remain, besides myself."

"And eight of my crew lie in graves on the beach," Captain Pérez added.

"The *San Jose* has never arrived?" inquired the priest. The others merely shook their heads.

Tears flooded the eyes of all the men gathered in the brushwood shelter. Junípero removed his misty spectacles, and wiped them. Then he fell on his knees and recited the age-old prayer of the Church for its dead, while the men joined in the responses.

"Dear friends," Junípero began as he rose to his feet after a long silence had fallen over the group, "a heavy blow has indeed fallen on our expedition. A few more than half the number who started on this glorious trek remain. We all knew, though, when we undertook it, that trials and hardships would be ours. We cannot alter the past. We can only accept the present, and push on to accomplish our task in the future."

At his words, a feeling of hope and confidence seemed to return to the men who had seen so much of horror in the past weeks.

After Mass the next morning, the leaders all met again to plan the course they should take. It was decided that the *San Antonio* should return to San Blas to bring back supplies, as well as a full crew for herself and the *San Carlos*. The sick were to remain in the hospital under the care of the doctor, Padre Serra, and the other friars, with some soldiers for protection. The *San Carlos*, with her captain, was to stay in port. All the others, under Governor Portolá, were to go by land to seek the port of Monterey. No time should be lost in planting a settlement there, Portolá insisted. Gálvez had made it clear that Spain's claim must be made secure. Who knew when other nations might decide to move in?

Just a week later, the sails of the *San Antonio* dipped beneath the horizon. With her went the prayers and hopes of the men gathered on the shore to watch her leave.

On an afternoon a few days later, Portolá, with Fray Crespi and another missionary, Captain Rivera, Sergeant Ortega, as well as most of the men well enough to begin the journey, moved on to the north.

Junípero watched them go with mixed feelings. He and Padres Parrón and Vizcaíno, Doctor Pratt, and Captain Villa were left with about fifty helpless sick men to care for. The soldier guard numbered only eight, and there were eight mission Indians. Their task would be a hard and dangerous one. There was disappointment, too, in not being among the first to look on the fabulous port of Monterey. He reminded himself, though, that he had come to California to start missions, and that was his important goal.

To this end, Junípero and his Franciscans began to prepare for founding the Mission of San Diego. As soon as the last soldier of Portolá's party was out of sight, he sent the mission Indians and some of the soldiers into the hills to gather brushwood. With this, a few sapling poles, and grass and tules for a roof, a good-sized hut was built for a chapel. A huge cross was also carved out of a straight tree trunk.

Two days after the expedition to Monterey had left, the cross was set up before the chapel, facing the bay. Junípero blessed the cross, the chapel, and the ground. Then he sang High Mass, to the music of musket shots and with the incense of their smoke rising in the still air. He also preached a fine sermon to the handful of

Spaniards well enough to sit up and listen. This was the founding of the first Franciscan mission in California, San Diego de Alcalá, on the morning of July 16, 1769.

Not an Indian was in sight. They came soon, however, but not to learn about the Christian religion. They came for the beads and other gifts the missionaries gave them, and to annoy the white men. Like their neighbors to the south, they would steal anything they could take, except food. Apparently, they thought the Spaniards' food was to blame for their sickness. Many times, though, they crept into the hospital huts to snatch the sheets and blankets from the beds of the sick men. One dark night they rowed out to the *San Carlos*, where they cut pieces from her sails, and carried off parts of the ropes. They came in groups, and stood just outside the stockade, imitating the Spaniards in all they did, and laughing at them. Once or twice, when the soldiers could stand the jeers no longer, they fired their muskets into the air. The Indians only mimicked the shooting, and continued to make fun of the men.

Finally, one morning about a month after the mission had been founded, they made an armed raid on the little settlement. Two of the soldiers had gone with Padre Parrón to the *San Carlos*. Two more had taken the horses to the river. The heathens chose this moment to strike.

Junípero and his brother Franciscans were in the chapel, where they had just finished saying Mass. They heard the sound of many feet, and looked out to see a crowd of painted Indians, all with their bows and arrows. Junípero went to the door, and saw several of the savages dashing from the hospital huts with clothing and sheets they had taken from the sick. Others were leaving the storehouse with arms full of supplies. When the soldiers tried to make them replace what they had stolen, the natives began to shoot arrows at them. The soldiers, with the two who had come back from the river, quickly put on their leather jackets, and prepared to defend the camp. They were joined by a carpenter, by José María, the servant boy, and a blacksmith. All now fired their muskets at the attackers.

At the sound of the shooting, Junípero fell on his knees, and began praying that the little party might be saved without loss of life. After a few minutes all seemed still. Padre Vizcaíno went to the door, and lifted the straw mat. Instantly an arrow pierced his hand. While Junípero was removing the arrow, José María rushed into the hut.

Falling on his knees at the friar's feet, he gasped, "Padre, give me absolution, for the Indians have killed me."

Junípero raised his hand over the boy, who at that moment fell dead, an arrow through his throat.

The Spaniards fired their guns again and again. Three of the attackers were killed, and many wounded. In terror they fled, leaving much of their loot behind.

Some days later they returned, unarmed, and begged the doctor to heal their wounds. "By all means," said Junípero, when Doctor Pratt looked at him questioningly. "Let us return good for evil. By so doing we shall not only fulfill the law of Christ, but perhaps gain the Indians' friendship, as well."

The good doctor, with the friars' help, began to remove bullets, and dress wounds. The injured all recovered, and did not annoy the Spaniards again.

Also, they did not come to listen to the missionaries tell them about the religion of Christ. The only exception was a fifteen-year-old boy, who, before the raid, had spent a great deal of time at the mission. Junípero tried, in every way he knew, to bring about this boy's friendship, for he hoped to teach him Spanish. In return, he wished to learn from him as much of the Diegueño language as he could. Often the padre would take the boy to a little knoll near the camp, where they would sit together looking at the view about them. Junípero would point to a nearby tree. "El árbol," he would say again and again until the boy could repeat it after him. Then the lad would give the Indian word, and Junípero would say it many times to fix it in his mind.

For some time the padre had been eager to baptize an Indian baby. If he could start just one child on the Christian road, he thought, the parents would come along with it, and soon others would become interested, too. He decided to ask his young friend to invite the parents of an infant to bring it to the mission to have water poured on its head, and become a child of God.

The boy did not understand at first. Junípero took him into the chapel, and pointed to a picture of the Christ Child. Then he went through the act of pouring water from the conch shell at the baptismal font, which had already been hopefully set up. Finally the boy was made to understand, and sent off to his people. A few days later he returned with a young savage painted with bands of red and blue, carrying his infant son, and accompanied by a large group of Indians.

Junípero was elated. The first baptism in the first mission of California! This was indeed an event. He had the child dressed in a baptismal robe brought from Mexico for just such an occasion. He invited all the Spaniards and mission Indians to the chapel, and asked the corporal of the soldiers to be the godfather.

The tiny chapel was filled with the few Spaniards and the close-packed painted bodies of the Indians. In the darkness the pagans' curious eyes darted from the priest to the infant held by the bulky soldier. An autumn wind from the sea rustled the thatch roof overhead, while Junípero's joyful voice intoned the prayers, and the corporal gave the responses. The priest dipped the shell into the font, and was just about to pour the water over the baby's head when the father snatched the child from the corporal's arms, and he and the other Indians fled. Shocked and startled, Junípero stood for a long time holding the conch shell in his hand, and staring out the door through which the savages had left.

His heart was filled with grief, and a cloud of sadness passed over his face. "My plan has failed," he said to himself. "All my hopes for the first baptism at Mission San Diego have come to nothing."

Sorrow and disappointment long remained with him, but there was no time to brood over the failure. Doctor Pratt and the two friars had fallen ill, and the hospital was still full of scurvy-ridden sailors. For long hours each day Junípero would talk and pray with the patients, trying to cheer them, and give them hope and a desire to get well. Often he would sit patiently with a bowl of gruel, trying to force the food into mouths too sore to eat it. Not a few times he was called in the waning hours of the night to give the Last Sacrament to a dying man. At length he became ill himself. His illness was not serious, though, and like the doctor and the other two friars, he recovered. For a long time his usual strength did not return, however.

As the months stretched on, a feeling of gloom rested heavily on the little camp. Nothing had been heard from Portolá and his expedition. The sailors continued to die from their disease, and there were now nineteen mounds in the graveyard. Not a single convert had been made, for the Indians refused to come to the mission. Even Junípero's hopeful spirits were dejected.

As dusk drew on after an especially wearing day, he walked along the shore of the bay, where the lifeless masts of the *San Carlos* criss-crossed the faint streak of sunset left in the sky. The cool breeze from the Pacific seemed to blow through his weary being. Seating himself on a smooth boulder, he listened to the rhythm of the waves as they beat on the sand. A memory stirred somewhere within his heart. From out of the past he recalled the message that the tireless waves had brought to him as he stood on the deck of the ship that had brought him to the New World so long ago. It was the message of confidence in the eternal presence of the Creator, whose heartbeats he was hearing in the beating surf. All at once his faith in the final success of the sacred expedition was renewed. Greater hardships, and even despair for a time, might come, he foresaw, but in the end there must be success. Was it not, after all, God's own work? The Heavenly Father would not forsake those who were doing it.

A few days later, a volley of musket shots echoed through the nearby hills. Everyone within the stockade ran out to meet their friends from Monterey. When the first greetings were over, Padre Serra counted the men. Thankfully, he saw that not one had been lost. All had, indeed, returned, but what a sorry looking group they were. Thin and hollow-eyed, many seemed too weak to walk. There was a definite odor of mules about the whole party.

"Our food gave out," said Portolá simply. "We were forced to kill some of our faithful mules, and eat them, as perhaps you can tell," he added with a wry smile.

"And Monterey?" Junípero asked eagerly.

Portolá looked away, his disappointment showing in the droop of his shoulders.

"We could not find it," admitted Fray Crespi.

"But the maps, and Vizcaíno's description—were they all wrong?" Junípero was unable to believe it.

"We found Point Pinos and the mountain Vizcaíno

called Santa Lucía, which rises back of it. All the land marks mentioned in the old books were there, but the port was not."

"It seems hard to believe," Padre Serra remarked. "How do you account for it?"

"Perhaps in more than a century and a half, the harbor has filled with sand," Portolá ventured. "At any rate, after exploring carefully, we raised a large cross on the beach near a giant oak tree."

Vizcaíno's oak, of course, thought Junípero, but said nothing.

Portolá went on, "We carved these words on the cross: 'Dig at the base, and you will find a message.' The message, a record of our expedition, we put in a bottle, and buried. The cross can be seen by a ship at sea. We also planted two other crosses on rocky headlands looking over the water."

"Our father, Saint Francis, showed us his port, though, Fray Junípero." Juan Crespi put in.

Joy shown in Junípero's face. "Tell me about it," he urged.

"Sergeant Ortega, with a small searching party, saw it first from a high hill. A few days later, we all viewed it. It is a great arm of the sea, lying some miles north of Point Pinos."

"One day our good Saint Francis shall have his mission there," Junípero promised.

That day seemed far off, though, for Portolá was thoroughly discouraged. The next morning he announced that they would have to return to Lower California.

"And leave our mission here when it has barely started?" asked the padre. "We cannot do that, Governor. We must try to find Monterey, and carry out our orders from Don José de Gálvez," he added firmly.

"The plain fact is, Your Reverence," Portolá replied,

101

"That we have food for only a month longer, even if we use it sparingly."

"When the *San Antonio* arrives - - -," Padre Serra began.

"The *San Antonio*!" Portolá interrupted. "It is long overdue now. She has gone to the bottom of the sea, no doubt, like the *San Jose*."

"I am sure the *San Antonio* will come in good time. We must be patient, sir."

"The men cannot go on without food. They are not Franciscans, who can live on one tortilla a day," Portolá said almost scornfully. "If we start now, there will be supplies enough to take us back to Velicatá."

"We cannot abandon the expedition now," Junípero went on doggedly.

"If we stay, we shall all starve, and the expedition will fail, anyway."

Junípero clenched his hands, and stood very straight, while in a quiet, firm voice he said, "You may all go, but I will remain, and Fray Crespi, I know, will stay with me."

Portolá looked at the two frail, stubborn Franciscans. He was forced to admire their faith, though he doubted their wisdom.

"Nevertheless, we must prepare to leave. If the *San Antonio* does not arrive by the 20th of this month, we have no other course, but to return," he said, turning on his heel, and leaving the friars standing at the door of the chapel.

It was March 10th. In nine days, on the 19th, the feast of Saint Joseph would be celebrated. There was just time for a novena to the patron of the expedition. Surely he who had brought them to California, and kept them thus far, in spite of hardships, sickness, and death itself, would not forsake them now. Limping painfully, the stalwart friar entered the chapel to begin nine days

Ship arrival at Mission San Diego, March 19, 1770. Courtesy of Bancroft Library

of special prayers to Saint Joseph.

Meanwhile, preparations went on to leave the camp. Boxes were packed, and rolls of equipment made ready. The animals were tended carefully to enable them to make the long trip back. There was an air of relief and cheerfulness among the soldiers.

Each morning and evening Junípero walked to the top of a knoll, and looked out to sea with anxious eyes. The calm waters seemed to smile at him, mockingly. Not a speck could be seen on their untroubled waves. Only the stark masts of the *San Carlos* loomed forlornly against the horizon. "Tomorrow," the padre would say to himself, and return to the chapel to beg the good saint to intercede with God to save the expedition.

103

The "tomorrows" came and went, though, and the time for departure drew near. The men were almost gay as they thought of leaving this unhappy spot which had seen so much trouble. Portolá's mind seemed to be made up. Only Junípero and the faithful Fray Juan believed that there was any possibility that the party would not turn back.

Finally, March 19th dawned chill and foggy. The Mass for the feast of Saint Joseph was attended by everyone. The rest of the day was spent in final preparations. Tomorrow they would leave!

Late in the afternoon Junípero walked with lagging step to his knoll. A frown was on his brow as he shook his drooping head from time to time. What did one do when hope was gone?

As he came to the top of the little hill, the mists began to lift. With sad eyes he watched the curtain of gray rise over the water. The jagged edges of the murky veil seemed to form a frame. And in the frame - - -? Could it be? Was that really a dark speck on the horizon, or were his eyes playing tricks on him? He adjusted his spectacles, and peered with all his might into the west. It was growing larger! It must be, it was — a sail!

Forgetful of his lameness, he ran down the hill and into the camp, shouting, "The ship! The ship!"

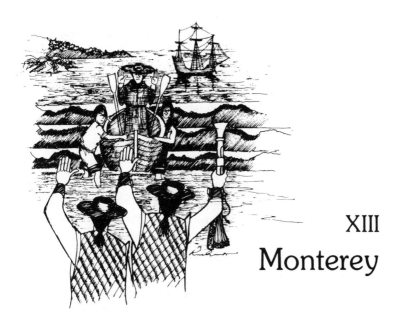

XIII
Monterey

The joy of the men at San Diego, as they watched the sails far out at sea, was soon turned to dismay. Instead of coming in to port, the ship moved on, and the sails disappeared in the fog. There was no doubt that it was the *San Antonio*. Of that they were sure. They guessed that the captain must be taking her to Monterey. Disappointed, they all turned wearily back to camp. Nothing more was said of leaving the next day, however, for they knew that relief would come to them soon. Somehow they would hold out until the ship came back.

Their faith was rewarded four days later, when the *San Antonio* quietly anchored in the bay. What a glad welcome for Captain Pérez and his crew! How good it was to see the boxes and barrels of supplies that filled the ship's hold!

"San Diego is saved!" shouted the soldiers.

"Monterey will be found!" exclaimed Portolá.

"The sacred expedition will succeed!" cried Junípero.

When Captain Pérez told his story, all were convinced that the watchful Saint Joseph had intervened, and that it was God's will that the expedition go on.

"I had orders from Don José de Gálvez to sail straight to Monterey," began Juan Pérez. "Both he and I thought that your party would be there, Governor Portolá."

"No," answered Portolá sadly. "We had to return, for we could not find Monterey."

The captain was amazed, but continued his story: When we reached the Santa Bárbara Islands, we had to put ashore for water. By signs, the Indians there told us that your expedition had come back south. At least, we thought that was what they were saying, but we could not be sure. At any rate, my orders were to proceed directly to Monterey. We started out, but when we were off Point Concepción, we lost an anchor. Knowing we should need it at Monterey, I gave orders to turn back to San Diego, where I could get another from the *San Carlos.*"

Captain Pérez looked at the faces about him. "And here I find all of you," he finished simply.

Almost at once Portolá began to prepare to push on to Monterey. There would be two expeditions. One was to go by land, led again by the Governor himself. The other was to approach by sea in the *San Antonio*, with Padre Serra in this group. San Diego would be held by two friars and a few soldiers.

Junípero sat on the cabin deck of the ship, his quill in hand, and an inkhorn nearby. While the *San Antonio* waited in the harbor for a good wind, he was writing to Francisco Palou, asking for news, wax candles for the altar, and for incense, forgotten in packing for the expe-

106

dition. He had had no word from his old friend for over a year. Junípero's thoughts went back to the voyage he and Francisco had undertaken together to the New World. How eager they had been then for the new life that was beginning for them. Many years had passed, and now Junípero was starting another voyage. He was just as eager for the new adventure as he had been then. Please God, it would be a fruitful one.

The *San Antonio* finally got under way, but her trip was a long one. When the winds blew, they brought fierce storms, which drove the ship southward; when they didn't blow, the *San Antonio* stood motionless. At length, however, on the evening of the last day of May, 1770, she entered a large bay.

Padre Serra stood with Captain Pérez on the bridge of the vessel. On the distant shore was a pin prick of light. As they sailed toward it, the light grew brighter, with points of flame leaping upward. "It is a watch-fire," exclaimed the captain. "Portolá and his men have arrived before us."

"And there is Monterey!" cried Junípero. "Of course it is. There are the two points of land guarding the egg-shaped harbor, just as Vizcaíno described them. There are the pines and cypresses growing along the shore. I am sure we shall find the other landmarks by tomorrow's daylight."

"I think you are right, Padre. Let us salute the land party." A rousing volley rang forth from the *San Antonio's* guns.

The next morning's sunlight shimmered the tranquil water, and brightened the curving beach, as a small boat from the ship sped toward the shore. Standing in the prow, his face alight with joy, was Junípero Serra. As he stepped ashore, Portolá and Fray Crespi hurried to meet him.

"Welcome to Monterey," shouted Portolá.

"Ah! You have found it this time," said Junípero.

"Yes. I think we must have been like men walking in a dream when we failed to see it before. Now our eyes are opened."

"Come," urged Fray Crespi, "and see for yourself. There," he said, pointing to a huge tree with branches spreading almost to the sea itself, "is Vizcaíno's oak. At high tide its branches really are washed by the waves, as he said."

"I knew it would still be here," declared Junípero.

"Over there beyond the water pools," went on Fray Juan leading the way, "is the ravine with its clear, cool water."

"Let us drink from it," suggested Junípero, "as Vizcaíno did."

When he looked around after stooping to drink from the cold crystal stream, Junípero saw a mammoth rock a short distance from the shore. On its sides smooth brown bodies caught the sunlight as they leapt and frisked about. "The seals are playing today, just as they did a century and a half ago," marvelled Junípero.

"Not the same ones, perhaps, Fray," laughed Juan Crespi.

"Their descendents, then," smiled Junípero. "Oh, this is Monterey, without a doubt."

"The real proof of it you have yet to see," remarked Fray Juan. "Come. From this spot the shape of the bay changes. What does it look like now?"

"Why, the letter 'o' just as Vizcaíno said," cried Junípero in triumph. "Monterey," he whispered.

Juan Crespi only nodded, and looked happily at the lovely scene. Blue and white lupines bowed above a rosy carpet of ice-plant on the dunes. The gnarled cypresses, bent into weird shapes by the wind, soared above the rocky cliffs, and looked down on the sapphire bay.

"Tell me, Fray," said Junípero eagerly, "have the pagans showed themselves to you?"

"Not yet, but we know they are about. When we first came upon the cross we had planted on the height over there," Fray Juan said, pointing toward Carmel Bay, "there was a ring of arrows with feather-tipped branches around it. A string of nearly fresh sardines hung from one branch of a nearby tree, and a piece of meat from another. At the foot of the cross was a little pile of mussels. We did not know what these things meant, but we felt sure the *Gentiles* had put them there."

"Without doubt," Junípero agreed. "Perhaps one day we shall find out."

Meanwhile, the men had begun to build a brushwood shelter under the oak. When it was finished two days later, and an altar set up beneath it, two of the finest toned bells were swung over a branch of the tree.

As the brave, clear tones of the bells rang out, the entire company from ship and shore gathered to take possession of the land for Spain, and to attend the Mass of thanksgiving. It was Pentecost Sunday, June 3rd, 1770. Padre Serra blessed the great cross which had been set up, and all knelt before it. He then sprinkled holy water over the site, and began High Mass before the altar, on which had been placed a lovely statue of Our Lady. At the Sanctus, the soldiers' muskets boomed out, their noise traveling over wooded hills and shining water. Junípero fancied that the sound was reaching his "brown brothers" miles away, and that the words it heralded, "Holy! Holy! Holy! Lord God of Hosts. Heaven and earth are full of Your glory. Hosanna in the highest," would somehow find a place in their pagan hearts. As he raised aloft the sacred Host, he had the feeling that he was elevating it not only to the Spaniards kneeling before

109

him, but to unseen thousands of "Gentiles" who would one day adore it. After Mass he declared the Mission of San Carlos Borromeo founded.

When the religious ceremonies were over, the flags of Spain were unfurled and saluted. Portolá took possession of the land in the name of the King of Spain. He uprooted some weeds, and threw them, with a few rocks, as far as he could. This meant that no other country could now claim the land. Monterey, dreaming idly in the sun for many scores of years, had become Spain's farthest outpost.

As the eventful day drew to a close, Junípero watched the purple shadows lengthen on the hills. A feeling of peace such as he had not known during the weary months at San Diego came upon him. Happiness lay upon his heart like a blessing. The place—this lovely place of cliffs and sea and hills—seemed to close about him, and tenderly enfold his being. How was it, he wondered, that coming to this fair spot, a spot he had never seen before, should be like coming home? It must be because it was the land so long desired, the dwelling place of his spirit, the home of his heart. This would, indeed, be "his" mission, as he and Gálvez had planned.

With the help of the mission Indians brought from Lower California, he began to build a rude chapel. Poles driven into the ground were interlaced with branches covered with mud. Bunches of grass tied together formed a thatch roof. A house for the missionaries was also built in this way.

Other building was going on, too. Captain Fages and his thirty soldiers were erecting their barracks, as well as warehouses for the supplies, and a stockade for protection. Fages was in command now, for Portolá, his work of planting colonies at San Diego and Monterey finished, had turned over his post to the young captain.

He would return to Mexico on the *San Antonio* when she left Monterey.

In the meantime, Junípero explored the nearby country. He had decided that a better spot for the mission could be found. The place where the chapel was being built, though beautiful, did not have enough fertile land around it for the fields where the mission crops would be grown. A lack of water, too, would make it hard to irrigate. Another reason, of which he spoke only to Juan Crespi, was that it was too near the soldiers' garrison. The guns of the soldiers would, he knew, frighten the Indians, and prevent their coming to the mission. A more compelling consideration had to do with the soldiers' molestation of the Indian women. It was clear that permanent propinquity would only increase this disturbing tendency.

Fray Juan led him through the pine woods to the place, about four miles away, among the green hillsides along the Carmel River, where the land party had camped, and where the arrows and food had been found at the foot of the cross. It was a lovely spot nestled beneath the Santa Lucía Mountains, above the cypress bordered headlands of Carmel Bay. Broad acres stretched about it for fields, while the river would furnish water for future crops. It was far enough from the presidio at Monterey to avoid trouble with the soldiers, and yet close enough to obtain protection if it were needed.

"It is the very place for 'my' mission," explained Junípero. "I shall write at once to the Viceroy and to Gálvez, asking for permission to move here."

In his letters, which were to go on the *San Antonio*, he also begged for more missionaries, and for the right to build a string of missions joining San Diego with the port of San Francisco, which Portolá's men had found, as well as for more supplies and equipment.

After the sailing of the ship, Junípero hoped to begin

the mission of San Buenaventura, for which Don José de Gálvez had packed the church supplies at La Paz. Captain Fages told the priest that he did not have enough soldiers to send to guard it. Hence, he had to postpone the building of this mission until a future date.

With Fray Juan's help, he began to spend all his time trying to get the Indians to come to San Carlos. Whenever they came near, he would give them presents of food and beads. These they would take, and disappear. Since neither he nor anyone else knew anything of their language, Junípero sadly watched them go. In time, one of the young mission Indians from Lower California began to learn a few words. The priest was delighted, and urged the boy to go among the *Gentiles* as often as he could. He felt that in this way God would open the door for converting them. Little by little the boy made the natives understand that the friars had come to teach them, and to lead them to heaven.

That Christmas, Junípero was able to bring to the Christ Child a truly worthwhile gift. The Kings of the East had brought gold and frankincense and myrrh to lay at the manger. This Franciscan padre brought a human soul to love the Holy Infant. On December 26th he baptized the first Indian in California.

After this, it was not long before others began coming to the mission. Nor was it hard to persuade them to accept the religious teachings of the friars. The reason for this they explained as soon as they could speak enough Spanish, and the Spaniards understood a little of their language. They said that when they first saw the white men, they noticed that they all wore shining crosses on their breasts. After they departed, the great cross they had left on the headland seemed to be lighted with brilliant beams, and to grow so large that it reached to heaven. The people were frightened, and brought offerings to this strange god. When it did not eat the offerings, they decided it meant them no harm, and so they placed the arrows at its feet as a token that they wished to make peace. After seeing these wondrous signs, they felt that they were meant to accept the padres' teachings.

Junípero never attempted to explain the matter of the lighted cross, but simply accepted it as one of the mysterious ways in which Heaven had seen fit to help in converting the pagans.

XIV

San Antonio
and
San Luis Obispo

On a clear day of wind and racing clouds, Junípero
stood on a rock-piled headland watching the dip and rise
of white sails as they entered the bay. There would
always be a lump in his throat and a thumping in his
chest when he saw those sails of the *San Antonio* afar
off. He could never forget what the sight of them had
meant on that foggy day in San Diego when they had
appeared in answer to his prayers. It was the saving of
California for Spain, and of her people for the Church.

Now, the good ship, serving as a supply vessel between
San Blas and California, rode once more into port. What
a cargo she carried! There were ten missionaries, lately
come from Spain. There were supplies and equipment in
abundance, and—wonder of wonders—the wax candles
and incense that Junípero had begged for so long. Bells

115

there were, too, and candlesticks, and a new set of vestments "golden and sumptuous" sent by the Viceroy especially for Padre Serra's Mission of San Carlos. Letters tumbled from the mail bags—letters from Francisco Palou and from his other Franciscan brothers, as well as permission from Gálvez and the Viceroy to locate San Carlos where he thought best, and to start five other missions.

When the new missionaries had been welcomed, and the letters read, Junípero went alone to the chapel. There he fell on his knees to thank the Heavenly Father for the favors brought him that day. Now, with the workers, the winning of souls in California could really begin. The hardships of the sacred expedition had been great, but always, when despair had been close at hand, Heaven had sent relief. At last those pioneer trials were over, and his real work could start. With overflowing heart, he gave his thanks to God.

After more than a month in port, the *San Antonio* left for San Diego with the friars who were to go to the southern missions. Junípero gave them his blessing, and then lost no time in setting out for the new site of "his" mission.

With him went some of the mission Indians, a few sailors, and a guard of soldiers. They were to begin felling trees from the thickly wooded hillsides for the mission buildings. As this would take some time, he left the men there, and set out to the southeast to found the Mission of San Antonio de Padua.

The two friars who had been assigned to the new mission went with him, as well as a guard of soldiers, and some mission Indians, while the mule train carried supplies. They journeyed toward the Santa Lucía Mountains. Just at the foot of the pine-clad hills they found a beautiful valley, whose floor was a wide plain. Oak

116

Mission San Antonio De Padua founded by Father Serra, July 14, 1771.

trees covered it thickly, and a river ran through it. The water raced deep and sparkling, even though it was midsummer, the height of the dry season.

It was July 14th, 1771, when Padre Serra told the party to stop on the banks of the river. The pack animals were unloaded, and a bell swung from a mighty oak tree. At once Junípero sprang to the rope end, and began pulling it as hard as he could, shouting, as the bell rang out, "Hear, Oh *Gentiles*! Come, Oh come to the Holy Church! Come, Oh come, and receive the faith of Jesus Christ!"

One of the missionaries said to him, "Padre, why do you tire yourself? This is not the place where the church is to be built, nor is there a *Gentile* in the vicinity. It is useless to ring the bell."

117

"Padre," the President of the Missions answered, "let me in this way relieve my heart, which wishes that this bell might be heard all over the world, or at least by all the pagan people who live in these mountains."

The cross was put up, a shelter of branches made, and an altar built under it. During the Mass which followed, as Junípero turned to his little group after the Gospel, he saw an Indian peering out from behind the oak tree. It was the first time that one of them had been present at the founding of a mission in California. "I trust that this mission will come to be a great settlement of many Christians," Junípero said, "for this pagan will surely tell his friends what he has seen."

When Mass was over, the padre gave the lone Indian a string of colored beads, and some figs. Soon other savages began to come, bringing gifts of pine nuts and acorns, which were their food. Within a few days, the pagans were coming regularly, showing the greatest trust in the friars because of their affection and kindness. They brought their store of acorns and seeds to be kept for them at the mission until winter.

The soldiers and mission Indians at once began cutting down trees to build houses for the mission and the stockade. Since the beginning of this mission seemed so favorable, Junípero stayed only two weeks.

Now that permission had been granted for the other missions, he could hardly wait to start them. Each day of delay, he felt, meant that some souls were being lost to God. He had hoped to begin San Luis Obispo at once, but soldiers for a guard could not be spared at Monterey. Therefore, he had to be content to wait until Fages, who was in San Diego, should return with more troops.

In the meantime, he went to the new site of San Carlos Mission. There he lived in a little shack of boughs, while he began carving a huge cross. When it was finished and set up in the middle of what was to be the courtyard, it was blessed. At daybreak each morning, and at sunset each evening, Junípero knelt before the cross, and it was there that the soldiers sang an early hymn.

"Amar a Dios (love God), my children," Junípero said as he made the sign of the cross over several Indian children who had come over from Monterey to see him. It was the old greeting that had echoed through the hills of Sierra Gorda when Padre Serra, as a young man, had taught his Indians at Jalpán to salute one another with these words. It was beginning to be heard now along the mission trails of California.

After the friar had knelt with the children before the cross, and prayed, he gave each of them a bowl of porridge made from boiled wheat and corn. Then, throwing an arm about the shoulders of the two nearest boys, he took them with him as he went to oversee the work being done on the buildings. Afterwards the young Indians sat on the ground about the "old padre," as they called him, listening to the stories of Christ's life, and helping him, by naming nearby objects, to learn their language.

As the sun in the west neared the end of its daily journey, the children joined their padre in prayers at the foot of the cross. Then they left to go back to Monterey, taking their leave with the same words they had used when they arrived, "Amar a Dios, Padre, Amar a Dios. A Dios — — Di — os—," died away as they vanished from sight around the curve of a hill.

At length, after several months, the buildings of the new mission site at Carmel were finished. Standing about the great cross-centered courtyard were the main structure, a separate kitchen, barracks for the soldiers, and a corral for the cows and other livestock. The principal building contained the chapel, the friars' rooms and office, and storage space for the food, farming implements, and gifts for the natives. It was made of woven twigs over a wooden framework, and plastered with mud. It had a mud roof, while the kitchen had thatch. A plot of ground was set aside for a vegetable garden, while around all was a stockade built of poles, with large gates which were locked at night.

On a day at the end of the year 1771, Junípero led Fray Juan, the two missionaries who were to go to San Luis Obispo, the new converts, and a guard of five soldiers through the piney crispness of the December woods from Monterey to the new mission. There, in its lovely location nestled at the foot of the hills above the curving sapphire bay, he established the headquarters of the California Missions, and the home of their President.

The gates of Junípero's mission swung open early in the new year to permit Captain Fages, just returned from San Diego, to enter. As military commander, the young captain now considered himself the most important person in California, and he rode in with great pomp. Junípero greeted him warmly, and begged for news of all that had happened in the south.

"After only a week of sailing," he began, "we arrived in the *San Antonio* at San Diego. The two padres who had asked to return to Mexico because of ill health, left. One went on the ship to San Blas, and the other with a land party. Padres Dumetz and Jayme at once took charge at San Diego."

"Our mission of San Gabriel—has it been started?" Junípero inquired eagerly.

"Yes," Fages replied, "though we had some trouble

*Mission San Luis Obispo de Tolosa founded by Father Serra,
September 1, 1772.*

there at first."

At the questioning look in Padre Serra's eyes, the
captain went on, "Just as we were about to start for
the new mission site, we discovered that ten of the
soldiers had deserted." A black look passed over Fages's
face. "I could not afford to lose them," he admitted,
"and so I had to ask Padre Paterna to go after them,
with a promise of full pardon, and bring them back.
That was not the end of our troubles with the soldiers,
though. Shortly after the expedition got under way, six
more left us. They returned one night later on, but only
to steal some cattle. The worthless wretches!" exclaimed

the captain, stamping his foot in a rage.

"You got them back?" asked the friar.

"I went after them myself, but when I found them, they resisted me with their guns, and hurled insults at me. I wished that I might leave them there in the wilderness, but with so few guards, that was not possible. I was forced to go back to San Diego to get Padre Dumetz to come and reason with them. He did so, and all returned."

"I do not understand why the soldiers wished to desert," said Junípero, remembering that no such thing had happened under Portolá.

"They complained of poor treatment. Of course, it is much better than they deserve—I consider myself very lenient with my men." Fages added.

Junípero made no comment, but began to wonder.

"In the meantime," Fages continued, "the two padres with ten soldiers and the mule train carrying the equipment, had gone on without me. On the bank of the Santa Ana River they found themselves suddenly surrounded by a band of yelling Indians, their bows with fixed arrows raised. Just when it seemed that the savages were about to attack, Padre Somera remembered a large altar painting of Our Lady of Sorrows that had come on the last supply ship, and was being taken to the new mission. Hastily taking it from the pack animal's back, he held it high over the heads of the howling warriors. The Indians, amazed, gazed at the sweet face of Our Lady, threw down their bows, and ran forward. Two chiefs took the strings of beads from their necks, and deposited them at the feet of the Blessed Mother. Then they left, only to return later with many more men, women, and children, who brought seeds and grain, which they piled before the picture, as they looked at it in awe."

"Our Blessed Lady had touched the *Gentiles'* hearts,

and brought about the change in them, of course," Junípero said. "To her we must give our thanks for the good beginning of the Mission of San Gabriel. Tell me, was the mission founded at once?"

"No," Fages replied. "The place was not suitable, so the padres went on until they found a better spot near a creek. Here on September 8th of the past year, 1771, the mission was begun with the usual ceremonies. The Indians helped to cut trees in an oak forest not far away, and to drag them to the mission site. They seemed to enjoy using the tools of our men, and to watch the buildings going up."

"It makes me very glad to know that this mission had such a happy beginning," remarked Junípero, with glowing eyes, "and that the natives had such friendly feelings for our people."

"At first, yes," said Fages, frowning, "but they soon showed themselves in a different light."

"How so?" asked Junípero.

"One day the chief of a nearby village led all his warriors against one of the soldiers who, with a friend, was out in a pasture with the horses. The soldier killed the chief, though, with a shot from his musket, and later our men cut off his head, and put it up on a pole as a warning to the savages."

Junípero's brow was furrowed as he asked, "Why was it that the *Gentiles* attacked this particular soldier, Captain?"

"I believe he had been guilty of molesting the chief's wife," Fages admitted.

"We can never win them to Christianity if the soldiers commit these crimes against them, and undo the effects of our teaching, by their bad example. I hope you punished the man, and let the Indians know that you had done so," said Junípero earnestly.

123

"The soldier was dealt with as I thought best," Fages insisted. "Soldiers are rough men, and cannot be expected to live like friars. I brought the man back with me in order to prevent more trouble."

The padre should have known that he had said enough, but his weakness for verbal combat with those whose views were opposed to his own led him to continue the argument.

"But unless crimes by our own Spaniards are not punished at once, and severely, we cannot convince the Indians that we have come to bring them good, not evil," he persisted.

"I could not afford to lose the services of a soldier when there are so few," said Fages in an irritated voice. "As it was, I had to increase the guard at San Gabriel, and hence there were not enough soldiers to send to San Buenaventura."

"It was not founded then?" asked Junípero. The huskiness of his voice showed his disappointment.

"No," said Fages tersely. "Eight soldiers were certainly not enough to protect the new mission."

"If the guilty soldier had been punished at once —," Junípero began.

Fages, rising angrily, interrupted, "You will please confine yourself to religious matters, Your Reverence, and I will attend to military affairs."

So saying, the Captain left, and rode haughtily out the mission gates.

XV
The
First
Journey
to San Diego

After Fages had left, Junípero sat long in the tiny mission office, his head bowed in thought. His spirits had been high of late, for it seemed that his dream of a line of missions running between San Diego and San Francisco might come true sooner than he had expected. Now he wondered. If Fages opposed him in all that he was trying to do, instead of working with him, it would be much harder, if not impossible. In any case, he could only be friendly and polite to the Captain, as the Franciscan rule obliged him to be, to try to curb his combative spirit, and to pray for help in dealing with him.

Later, when the padre asked for enough soldiers to send as a guard so that San Luis Obispo could be founded, Fages again refused. He said that if the Indians at San Gabriel should cause trouble again, he would need all his troops to go to the aid of the mission there.

With so much to be done in the new land, Junípero could not bear the idea of remaining idle. He suggested, therefore, that an expedition be sent to explore the country around the port of Saint Francis to find a good site for the mission, and to make friends with the *Gentiles* who lived there. Somewhat to the friar's surprise, Fages agreed to the idea. The truth was that the Captain had shortly before received orders from the Viceroy to do this very thing. Padre Serra sent Fray Juan Crespi to go on the trip, along with Fages himself, a dozen soldiers, and the necessary pack mules.

One morning while they were gone, Junípero was working in the vegetable garden at Carmel. With his gray robe tucked up, he had been showing his Indians how to pull the weeds from around the young plants. Now the converts were working in another part of the patch, while Junípero bent lovingly over the green shoots. A bright spring sun had sent the last wisps of morning fog scampering from the garden. The good smell of the damp, warm earth as he crumbled it in his fingers, took him back to his boyhood. For a moment he was little Miguel Serra, weeding his father's upland field, wondering as he used to do, how the warm earth, bright sun, and cool water could change tiny hard seeds into green living plants. The warm sun beating on the back of his neck made him drowsy. He caught himself thinking that soon he could run home for his mid-day bowl of thick soup, and a nice long siesta. With a jolt he came back to the present, and his laugh rang out as he thought of the difference between the aging Franciscan in his mission garden in California and the undersized boy on a hillside farm in Majorca. A lifetime and half the world lay between, but the miracle of nature still went on. The little rock-like seeds from Mexico had sprouted and grown in their new home, and gave promise of a fine

Father Serra at Carmel Mission.

crop. He stood and looked proudly at the brave stalks of beans and corn, and peppers standing straight and tall in their neat rows. He could not know how soon they would play a part in sustaining the life of his mission.

At the "plof plof" of hoofbeats on the road, he turned to see a horse and rider approaching the gates. Hastily pulling down his robe, he went to meet the visitor. "Ah, news from San Diego," he called, as he recognized the messenger.

"Not very good news, I fear, Your Reverence," said the man, handing Junípero a letter. "There is little food left, and the people at both San Diego and San Gabriel are in danger of starving if they do not get help."

Junípero's eyes traveled swiftly over the letter. The supply ships were late in arriving. The new Indian converts made many more mouths to feed. The supplies would soon be gone. Padre Dumetz had gone to Lower California to get help from the missions there.

127

The Father President at once sent a messenger to find Captain Fages. When the commander returned, a mule train loaded with food was sent to the southern missions. This meant a shortage of provisions for Carmel, the presidio at Monterey, and San Antonio, but it was hoped that the ships would arrive soon.

The weeks dragged on, though, and no vessels appeared. When the food supplies were gone, the padre was able to give his people vegetables from his mission garden, and milk from his mission cows. There was not enough, though, to prevent the pains of hunger. Junípero never thought about himself, for, in his Franciscan way, he had learned to eat only enough to keep body and soul together. It pained him, however, to see the Indian converts going hungry. They had been led to give up their wild life, and accept the ways of civilization, and now he was not able to give them enough to eat. The *Gentiles* themselves soon helped out by bringing to the mission seeds and acorns from their pagan friends.

It was Captain Fages who finally kept them all from starving. Leaving a few soldiers at the presidio for protection, he took the rest of his troops on a hunting trip. They went into the mountains to a place called Cañada de los Osos (Valley of the Bears), which was a breeding place for the animals. There the men stayed for three months, and killed so many of the beasts that they sent back twenty-five mules laden with the meat, and with seeds they had traded from the Indians they met. Now it was hoped that there would be enough food to last until the supply ships came.

One day in the late summer, the Father President received a letter from San Diego from his old friend, Juan Pérez, Captain of the *San Antonio*. Both his ship and the *San Carlos* were in port with their cargo of supplies, he wrote. They had tried to go to Monterey, but strong winds had driven them back. Therefore, the provisions would have to be taken north by pack animals.

At Monterey Junípero stood looking at the mules in the corral. They, too, were suffering from lack of food, and from the effects of the hard trip to the Valley of the Bears. "The beasts are nothing but skin and bones," he said to Captain Fages. "They are in no condition to bring back heavy loads all the way from San Diego."

Fages agreed. "The ships are our only hope," he said firmly. "They must come to Monterey."

Junípero considered. If only he could talk to Captain Pérez, he was sure he could persuade his old friend to try once more to reach the northern port. Moreover, he wanted very much to start the Mission of San Luis Obispo, and the long-delayed San Buenaventura. Suddenly, he seemed filled with a new energy, and a glow came to his eyes. "I shall go to San Diego myself," he cried, "and talk to Juan Pérez."

"And I shall go with you," said Captain Fages.

Late in August the two set out with Padre Cavaller, a guard of soldiers, and a train of pack mules with the church supplies, the farm tools, and furnishings for the new mission.

On the way they stopped at San Antonio, where a number of Indian converts came out to meet them. "Amar a Dios, old padre," came the greeting down the trail.

The Father President was hoarse with emotion as he answered this loving welcome on his first mission visit in California, "Amar a Dios, my children."

He found that here, as at Carmel, the kindly Indians had brought in food to the mission to relieve the famine. They would make good Christians, he thought, as his heart rejoiced to hear that more and more of them were being converted.

129

About seventy miles from San Antonio, the party came to the Valley of the Bears. They were surrounded by friendly pagans who were grateful to the white men for killing the bears, of which they were much afraid.

On the first day of September, 1771, on a low hill overlooking the valley, Padre Serra said Mass in a brush-wood shelter in front of a large cross he had set up, and founded the mission of San Luis Obispo de Tolosa. Five soldiers and two Christian Indians were left with Padre Cavaller, as well as a scanty supply of provisions—all that could be spared.

It was, perhaps, not a very favorable beginning, but it marked the start of another Christian outpost in the wilderness. As Junípero continued on his journey the next day, and looked back at the rude shelter, he happily counted off half a chaplet of fat beads on his rosary. Five missions had now been founded in California. Soon, he hoped, San Buenaventura would make the sixth.

As the party neared San Gabriel Junípero tried to hurry them on. He was eager for a view of this mission he had yet to see. Soon, standing on a hilltop, he looked down at a fair valley with a rushing creek bordered by cottonwoods and willows. On the hillsides above it were wild blackberries and vines heavy with clusters of grapes. Close by the stream were the mission shelters made of poles and brush with grass roofs. Junípero counted ten huts grouped around the main ones. These would be for the converts, he knew, and rejoiced that a few, at least, had been brought into the Church at this mission whose beginning had been so unhappy.

When he talked to the two padres there, the Father President found that peace had still not come to San Gabriel. The extra troops that Fages had stationed there had only terrified the natives. The soldiers were an unruly lot, who would ride among the Indians, lassoing the women, and shooting the men who went to their aid. This, of course, made it hard for the friars to get the pagans to come near the mission. Junípero appealed to Fages to control the troops, but the commander only shrugged, reminding the priest that he, Don Pedro Fages, was in charge of military matters.

Much as he regretted the captain's refusal to take his advice in controlling the soldiers, the Father President was not disheartened. He asked Our Lady of Sorrows, whose loving face had calmed the warlike spirit of the Indians there, to take the mission under her care. So sure was he that San Gabriel would grow, that he left with the missionaries a large book in which to record the baptisms performed there.

Then, though his foot pained severely, he went on without stopping to rest, and in a few days reached San Diego. At once he set about trying to convince Juan Pérez, captain of the *San Antonio*, that he must try to get to Monterey with the supplies.

"It is well-nigh impossible to transport enough provisions for three missions and a presidio by land, Juan," he began. "It is a journey of over four hundred miles, and our mules are too few and too weary to carry the heavy loads. Moreover, it costs much more to take the freight overland, and it takes a great deal longer. Besides, the mule trains must pass through unfriendly pagan country, and we are without soldiers for a sufficient guard."

"But, Your Reverence, both the *San Antonio* and the *San Carlos* reached the latitude of Monterey, and my ship was actually only a few miles offshore, but the winds were so severe that we could not make port."

"You must try again, my friend, for if you do not, I fear that our three northern missions may be lost. The suffering among our people for want of food was great.

It was, in part, the reason for the desertion of fifteen soldiers from Monterey. There is danger that more may leave, and take up life among the pagans, if they do not soon get relief from the shortage."

"The season is already far advanced," Pérez answered, "and winter would probably arrive while we were at Monterey, if we got there. Our ships are not built to withstand the storms of northern winters."

"Will you not trust in our Lord, Juan?" asked Junípero. "You will be sailing in His service, and you may be sure that the Heavenly Father will not allow the weather to interfere with His work."

Juan Pérez was silent for many moments. At last he said, "I cannot refuse to make a voyage that will help in the Lord's work. Pray for our success, Your Reverence, and I will begin getting ready at once to sail for Monterey."

"My prayers will go with you," Junípero assured him.

Having succeeded in this step, he turned his thoughts to the Santa Barbara region, where there were so many Indians who should be brought into the Church! He would take along all the equipment packed four years before by Don José de Gálvez for the mission he had called his own. But when Junípero asked Fages for a guard to take with them, the commander flatly refused. Moreover, his refusal seemed to mean that he would not consent to the starting of any more missions in the future. To add to this outrage, the commander showed the Father President part of a letter from Antonio Bucareli, the new Viceroy. It stated that Fages was to impress upon Padre Serra that he and all others were to obey the captain's orders.

This letter made it clear to Junípero that the new Viceroy, miles away in Mexico City, did not understand the situation in California, and that the Governor's reports had not presented the missionaries' views. Something must be done at once to make this new official understand that the missions were the most important part of the work here, and that it was the duty of the military to help, not hinder, in their founding.

He discussed the whole matter of Fages's conduct with the other Franciscans. He told them of letters to him which had been delayed in delivery, and even opened; he told of supplies held at the presidio; he reminded them of refusals to permit soldiers to help with the mission work.

Padre Jayme was the first to speak. "The Viceroy must be told of the real situation here," he said earnestly.

"Someone must go to Mexico City to confer with him," agreed Padre de la Peña.

All eyes were turned on Junípero. He was the oldest of the friars, frail and lame, and weary from the journey he had just made. Somehow he was shabbier than all the others. But in his eyes still glowed the fire that had led them all on this great adventure to California.

"The Father President is the one who can best plead our cause in Mexico," said Padre Jayme, adding, "if he feels able to make the trip."

"The good God will give me strength," was the familiar answer.

XVI
To
Mexico
City

An autumn haze lay over the russet hills bordering the wide bay of San Diego as Junípero stood on the deck of the *San Carlos*. He was sailing for San Blas on the first stage of his journey to Mexico City. Beside him, Juan Evangelista, a boy of fifteen, one of the first Indians to have been baptized at Monterey, gazed in wide-eyed wonder as he felt the motion of the ship, and saw his native shore line fading into the distance. He was a bright lad, who had learned to speak Spanish, and was much devoted to the "old padre." Junípero, nearing his sixtieth birthday, was happy to be able to have this handsome, strong, young boy make the trip with him so that he could show the officials in Mexico a sample of the missionaries' work in California.

The voyage began on October 20th in the year 1772. A fortnight later it ended when the ship came into the port of San Blas. From there the journey would be nearly six hundred miles by land.

As he limped down the gangplank, the padre heard the single sound of a hammer beating on metal, then silence. Looking around, he saw that a ship was being built at a shipyard nearby. "Come," he said to Juan, "let us go aboard this new vessel."

He was surprised to see that of the many builders standing around, only one or two were working. Jokingly, he spoke to them. "If you do not work harder," he said, "this ship will not be ready to take me back to San Diego when I return from Mexico."

The foreman stepped up and answered him, "I am afraid you will not do that, Your Reverence, as an order has been received to stop work, for no more ships are to sail from this port for California."

The rumors he had heard that San Blas was going to be abandoned as a supply port were true, then. He had come just in time, he thought, for that must not happen. He would have to convince the Viceroy that the missions in California could not go on without San Blas as a provision base.

"I intend to see that the order is changed when I reach Mexico City," Junípero told the workmen, "and I wish to return in this vessel."

At this the foreman shook his head, and the workers laughed, little dreaming how it would all turn out.

While at San Blas, Junípero also heard the news that the Dominican Order had taken over all the missions in Lower California. When he arrived at Tepic, he found two missionaries from that finger of land. Some of the Franciscans who had been at missions in Lower California, including themselves, were going back to their College of San Fernando, they told him. Others were to be sent to Upper California.

"Padre Francisco Palou —," Junípero went on eagerly, "Where is he to go?"

"To California, if he wishes to go there," answered the friars.

Junípero lost no time in writing to Francisco urging his old friend with whom he had first come to the New World, to join him in California. "If you decide that we are to live and die there together, it will be for me the greatest of consolations, but Your Reverence should do as God may direct you, and I shall be resigned to the Divine Will," he wrote.

Hopeful that Francisco would be near him in the future, he started for the capital city. The journey, over rough trails, was long and arduous. At Guadalajara, less than half way, both he and the Indian boy became very ill with typhoid fever. For a time it seemed as if neither of them would live, and they received the last rites. Junípero prayed without ceasing for Juan, however. He did not fear death for himself, but he did fear that the Indians of Monterey would never trust the Spaniards again if the boy died while he was among them. The prayers were answered, for both the aging priest and the young convert recovered.

When they were well enough, they began the last stage of the journey, only to have Padre Serra fall sick again at the College of the Holy Cross in Querétaro. Once more he was at the point of receiving the last rites, when the fever suddenly left him, and he regained his health enough to go on. Finally, early in February of 1773, he arrived at the well-remembered gates of San Fernando, looking very tired, worn, and thin.

He was once again in the greatest city of New Spain, but he would have been scarcely aware of its splendor had not Juan been with him. The Indian boy, who a few years before had been chasing rabbits in the California wilderness, stared unbelievingly at the huge buildings of stone, the wide cobbled streets, and the elegantly dressed people. He never tired of watching the glittering parade of coaches and horsemen on the paseo, or of gazing at the shops with their stock of clothing, food, and beautiful furniture.

Junípero, however, lost no time in asking for a meeting with Viceroy Bucareli. The great man listened to his story with respect and interest. He asked the Father President to put in writing the things he wished to have done, but agreed to have supplies sent at once from San Blas to the needy missions.

Back at San Fernando, Junípero began his report. He listed thirty-two points for the general welfare of the missions, besides giving the reasons why San Blas should not be abandoned as a supply base.

He had to wait two months while a Council of War and State discussed his report. When the answer came, he found to his joy, that many of the things he had asked for had been granted. Important among them was the understanding that the padres alone had the right to control the mission Indians in the same way that a parent controls his children. Another was that the military commander was to remove, at the padres' request, any soldier who was a bad example to the natives. Commander Fages was to be replaced by Captain Rivera y Moncada, who had led the first land expedition to San Diego. Captain Anza was directed to open up a land route from Sonora in Mexico to the missions, as Padre Serra had advised. This would be a help in getting more settlers to go to California. San Blas was to remain as a port of supply. In addition to granting his requests, many gifts of food, church supplies, implements, clothing, and presents for the Indians were given the Father President of the Missions of California.

138

Joyful in the knowledge that his trip had been successful, Junípero would have returned to his beloved Indians
at once, except that Juan Evangelista was to receive
the Sacrament of Confirmation.

Standing behind the redskin youth as his sponsor while
the boy knelt at the altar, Junípero felt tears of joy
spring to his eyes. Here in the Archbishop's own house
chapel, the first California Indian was becoming a
"soldier of Jesus Christ." In this moment of triumph,
the careworn padre felt that all the hardships and suffering of the sacred expedition had been worthwhile.

On the return journey, Junípero had the company of
another Franciscan who was going to California. Health
and good fortune were with them, for they reached the
coast safely. It was late in January of the year 1774
before the ships were loaded and ready to sail.

As he was boarding the new ship, the *Santiago*, the
builders' foreman came up to Junípero. "Father President," he said, "your prophecy has been fulfilled, and
you are really to sail in this new ship, as you said you
would.

"Let us thank God for granting our desire. I want to
thank all of you, also, who have worked so hard for the
sake of the poor people of Monterey."

The *Santiago* was to have gone directly to Monterey
with supplies to relieve the shortage there. It was discovered that minor repairs were needed, though, and she
made for the port of San Diego, instead.

On an early spring morning Junípero stood on the
deck, peering into the distance across the sun-touched
water. Gradually he became aware of two gray-green
lines afar off. As he gazed, they grew heavier and clearer,
and merged into the outlines he remembered. With a full
heart he thought of what lay beyond them—the hills,
the forests, the lush valleys of California, peopled with

the "brown brothers" for whom the remaining years of his life would be spent. These were the shores of his beloved land. Please God, he would never leave them again!

How good it was to receive the loving welcome of the padres at San Diego, and to see the many new Christians who had come to the mission since he left. He went about among them, touching their foreheads with the sign of the cross, and putting his arm about their shoulders.

He was distressed, though, to hear the stories of the famine which had lasted so long, for the ship sent by Bucareli, at Junípero's request, had never been able to land. The Father President resolved to return by land to Monterey, so that he might visit each mission to see for himself how it had fared, and to thank the missionaries for staying at their posts during the time of want.

San Gabriel was still humming with excitement caused by the arrival of Anza's expedition a week or so before. Junípero had heard about that amazing trip when a pack train from San Gabriel had come to San Diego to get supplies from the *Santiago*. In fact, Fray Garcés, who had gone along with the group, returned to San Gabriel with the Father President.

"You cannot imagine our surprise," Padre Lasuén of San Gabriel told Junípero, "when Captain Juan Bautista de Anza and his party stumbled into our courtyard here at San Gabriel just at sunset one day in March. They were on the verge of starvation, tired and footsore, after their journey of seven hundred miles from Sonora, Mexico."

"I knew that Captain Anza could break the trail, if anyone could," Junípero said. "I saw some of his men at San Diego. How many were in the party, all told, Padre?"

"Twenty-four, including the two friars, Fray Garcés and Fray Díaz. The two missionaries gave me a new robe, hood, and sandals. My old ones had been patched until they barely hung together. I was almost in the same state as the Indians," laughed Padre Lasuén.

"Perhaps, Padre, your mission here will be host to many more travelers who will come from Mexico along the trail they have blazed," Padre Serra said.

"I hope we shall be able to give them a better welcome than these first ones," Padre Lasuén murmured. "The famine had left us with scarcely any food to offer the hungry people. However, we rang the church bells as a sort of salute, and sang the 'Te Deum' as well as a special Mass of thanksgiving, and gave them a place to rest. As you know, four of the men went down to San Diego, and brought back supplies from the *Santiago*, so we had a feast at long last."

"And where is the captain now?" Junípero wanted to know.

"He left here for Monterey to see you," the padre told him.

"Our paths will surely cross," Junípero stated. "How eager I am to meet this brave man!"

Trudging along the trail near the Santa Bárbara Channel in the late afternoon, Junípero with his soldier guard and Juan Evangelista, saw a cloud of dust ahead of him, and heard the sound of horses' hoofs. He guessed rightly that it was Anza. The captain dismounted from his horse as soon as he came in view, and walked to meet Junípero. For a long minute the two pioneers looked at each other. Then, at the padre's smile, Anza spoke. "I have been all the way to Monterey to meet the man who was responsible for my being sent by the Viceroy to blaze a trail from Sonora to the sea. And now I find you here on the road. I want to thank you, Your

141

Reverence, for your faith in me."

"It was a faith well placed, as your successful expedition has proved," Junípero answered. "I am very eager to hear all about that trip."

Through the hours of the soft spring night, the Father President heard with intense interest the story of the two months' journey from Tubac, Sonora. Anza told of the Apache raid which took some of his men and cattle at the very beginning. Then he spoke of the appearance of an Indian named Tarabal, who had run away from San Gabriel Mission, made his way to Sonora, and now consented to be the party's guide. The trip over the hot sands of the Mexican desert was a hard one, but the travelers were helped on the way by Palma, the Chief of the Yuma Indians, a partly civilized tribe of the Colorado River region. In the Colorado desert they were lost for some days. Their food ran short, and many of the men were almost exhausted, but they refused to turn back. Finally, they found a pass through the mountains, and dropped down to the fertile valley below, where at length, they reached the gates of San Gabriel Mission.

"Do you think the route can be used to bring settlers to California?" Junípero asked when the story was finished. "It is my belief that if Spain is to hold this region, we must have families—women and children as well as men, who will come here to make their homes."

"Now that we have made a trail around the sand dunes of the desert, it will be a fairly easy trip for hardy colonists. I hope soon to be able to bring the first group of settlers for San Francisco. I go now to make such a report to the Viceroy."

"God speed you, and keep you," called Junípero as the captain rode off toward Mexico City.

At San Luis Obispo there were three missionaries now, for Francisco Palou (who had, of course, chosen to come

142

to California when the Franciscans left Lower California) had brought two with him. He had also brought some Christian Indians to teach farming and weaving. Even so, there were only a few more than a dozen converts there. However, the first crops had been very good. The padres thought that they could attract many more Indians to the mission with gifts of wheat, beans, and corn. Junípero left with a hopeful feeling for the future of this mission.

San Antonio de Padua was no longer on the banks of the river. The stream had run dry, and the crops the padres had planted had died. The summer before, they had decided to move to a better location about three miles up the valley, near a swift-flowing creek. There the new church was being built of adobe bricks, which Padre Sitjar had taught the mission Indians to make.

As soon as Junípero had greeted the missionaries, and blessed the converts, who numbered one hundred sixty-three at that time, he went to watch the brick making. Some of the Indians were breaking up the clay soil, working it until it was fine and smooth, and placing it in holes in the ground. Others brought water from ditches dug from the creek. The water was poured in with the clay and some chopped straw or grass. Then one of the workers began treading the muddy mass with his bare feet. When it was well mixed, the adobe mud was put into wooden molds. As soon as it was dry enough to be taken out, it was removed and placed in the hot sun to harden.

"It will take us a long time to make enough bricks for all the buildings we shall need here," said Padre Sitjar, "but they will last for a long time."

"We shall some day have adobe buildings at all the missions," promised Junípero.

The last miles of his journey seemed unusually long,

for he was eager to reach his own mission at Carmel. It had suffered more than any other from the famine, he knew. Now, he could hardly wait to be there to see for himself how things were.

As he hastened toward Monterey, he saw two familiar figures coming along the road. Fray Francisco Palou had been serving as President of the California Missions in his absence. He hadn't seen the good friar since that day in Lower California when Francisco had bid him "Goodbye until eternity." Eternity, indeed! Junípero, seeming younger and in better health than he had five years before, sped over the trail so that young Juan Evangelista had to run to keep up with him. With Francisco was Fray Juan Crespi, Junípero's companion at San Carlos. Their eyes were brimming with tears of joy at the reunion. They threw their arms about the others' shoulders and for a few minutes they could find little to say to one another.

Later, Junípero heard how for eight months those at San Carlos had lived on milk and a sort of mush made of mashed peas with a little milk. The converts had been sent to the woods and beaches to find their own food.

"I was ashamed not to be able to give Captain Anza so much as a cup of chocolate for his breakfast," Fray Francisco said. "For a long time we had had nothing but a little coffee in the morning."

"Now that the *Santiago* has come to port at last," went on Fray Juan, pointing to the ship in the harbor, "we have plenty, and our Indians are coming back to the mission."

"My trip to see the Viceroy was so successful, and such good arrangements have been made, that I hope we shall never again have famine in California," Junípero assured his friends.

Then, with a sense of deep peace in his soul such as

he had not known for years, Padre Serra set out with his two dear friends on the five miles that led to home. The crunch of pine needles underfoot was like a glad welcome in the hush of the scented woods. The great oaks and wind-tossed cypresses with their thick webs of hanging gray moss all were pointing toward his beloved mission. Now and again the sound of the waves brought their message of the Almighty Heart ever beating for Its creatures.

And then, at last, Carmel! What place could be more heavenly in the May twilight—with the blue dusk sifting down on the folded hills, the drift of perfume from the closing petals of wild flowers on a nearby slope, and the sweet notes of the Angelus bringing the day's toil to a close? It was home, and the dearest place on earth to him.

XVII Revolt at San Diego

"If I were ten years younger, nothing would keep me from making this voyage of exploration myself," the Father President said with regret, as he gave his blessing to the ships and crew. The *Santiago* and the *San Antonio* were leaving on a day in June, 1774, to sail up the northwest coast to explore the shore line, and to look for possible sites for missions to be built there. Junípero's desire to bring the cross to all his "brown brothers" who lived up and down the shores of the Pacific, never faltered. He was happy to have this expedition set out, and though he was not to go himself, he sent Fray Juan Crespi. He knew that his good friend would keep a record of all that happened, and be able to tell him about the pagan people he saw on the voyage.

The ships returned late in August, not having been able, because of bad weather, to go as far north as the

Viceroy had ordered. The explorers had seen many Indians, though.

During the early autumn evenings at San Carlos Mission, Junípero never tired of hearing Fray Juan tell how the pagan people had come out to the ships in their canoes to trade blankets, furs, and woven mats for beads, ribbons, and clothing.

"We cannot let them perish without hearing the word of God," the head of the missions would say. "Some day, when it is possible, we must send missionaries to them.

Before long, Junipero saw Fray Francisco leave on an exploring trip, too. With Captain Rivera, the new military commander, and some soldiers, and a pack train, he set out to search for a good spot for the mission that was to be his near the port of Saint Francis.

"We planted the cross at two places on the huge bay," Fray Francisco said when the party returned. "We had to leave before exploring as much of it as we wished, though, for the rainy season had begun, and traveling was difficult."

These explorations of little-known places were of great interest to Junípero because they would be useful for the future. Nevertheless, he had before him always the wish to start more missions along the already well-traveled route from San Diego northward, at places where there were many Indians. Though no new troops had arrived, he urged Captain Rivera to take one or two soldiers from missions where they could be spared, so that a new one could be founded between San Diego and San Gabriel, to be called "San Juan Capistrano." Rivera agreed, and the two Franciscans who had been at San Carlos started out with the equipment.

Junípero always wished that he might be present at the founding of all the missions, but that could not be. He reflected, as he watched the little party march down

The slaying of Father Luis Jayme, O.F.M., at San Diego,
November 5, 1775.

the road from San Carlos, that in two months' time, perhaps, he would hear about the actual beginning of this new one. A message was to come, to be sure, but a different one from what he had imagined.

Late one night, as the pale winter moonlight wrapped the hills and shore in a silvery blanket, the mission stillness was broken by the sound of hoofbeats on the road. As the soldier guard swung open the gates, Captain Rivera himself rode in. Junípero, who usually spent much of the night in prayer and study, was awake, and hastened to the door. A glance at the captain's face told him at once that something was wrong.

"Bad news, Your Reverence," the commander said in a strained voice. "At San Diego the Indians have attacked and burned the mission."

"Have any of our people been lost?" asked Fray Francisco, who, with Fray Juan Crespi, had entered the

149

room in time to hear the commander's words.

"A blacksmith and a carpenter were killed fighting the pagans, and Padre Jayme has been murdered," Rivera answered in a low voice.

Fray Francisco's face paled, and he clutched his crucifix, while Fray Juan cried out in a stricken tone, but Junípero stood perfectly silent. After the first shock of the captain's words, a glow came to his face, and his eyes lit up. To him, the most important thing in the world was the saving of souls, and a priest who gave his life for that cause, had the happiest of deaths. Ever since his earliest missionary years, he had hoped for a martyr's death, himself. Now such a death had come to one of his friars. It was a moment of near-rejoicing, not of sorrow. "Thanks be to God," he burst out, "that the soil has now been watered with blood. We shall now see that the Indians of San Diego will all be converted. Tomorrow we shall honor the dead padre."

Captain Rivera had not expected such an outburst. For a moment he seemed startled, but then he handed the Father President a letter. "It is from Padre Fuster," he said, "giving all the details."

In a voice that was quiet, but charged with feeling, Junípero read aloud the letter which told of the ghastly happenings at San Diego more than a month before. It began with a reminder that a year before, the mission had been moved some five or six miles from the presidio because of better soil for crops. There was no stockade around the new buildings, and no soldiers stood guard at night.

Padre Jayme and Padre Fuster had been especially happy when, a short time before, sixty Indians has asked to be baptized. The day following the baptism, two brothers had run away, and could not be found. Rumors came to the mission that the runaways were going about among the villages arousing the natives by saying that they had been forced to become Christians. The padres thought little of these tales, however, and felt perfectly secure.

On the night of November 4th, Padre Fuster awoke to the wild shrieks of attacking savages, and the crackling of flames in the thatch roofs and wooden walls of the church and other buildings. Before setting the fires, the Indians had stolen all the church furnishings, and the priests' vestments. Then, as the fires blazed, they began their hideous yells, waving their war clubs, and fixing arrows in their bows.

Padre Fuster had the young son and nephew of Captain Ortega, commander of the San Diego garrison, in his charge. He at once took them to the barracks where the four soldiers and the carpenter were firing at the attackers. Indian arrows soon felled the carpenter, whose last words were, "Oh, Indian who has killed me, may God forgive you." One of the two blacksmiths was killed in his shop, but the other escaped, and joined the soldiers.

The barracks was now afire, and the Spaniards ran to the padres' house, where they tried vainly to find Fray Luis Jayme. This brave man, in the meantime, had gone out to speak to the savages. In his kindly way he had begun, "Amar a Dios, my children," whereupon the howling mob sprang upon him. They dragged him to a dry creek bed, tore off his robe, beat him with clubs and stones, and fired arrows into his dying body.

The white men and boys finally took refuge in an adobe kitchen. The corporal of the soldiers was the only one not wounded by this time, and he alone was able to fire a gun, though some of the others helped him load and unload the muskets. He shouted orders to the men in a loud voice, though, as if they were all firing, so that the Indians would not know that only one man was fighting them. Burning arrows were finding their mark in the dry thatch of the roof above, and the flaming grass showered down into the room. A bag of gunpowder lay on the floor. Padre Fuster threw himself on top of it, and spread his robe out to keep the flames away.

So the horrible night wore on, but by morning the attackers had left. As soon as they were gone, the Indian converts came to look for the padres. They said they had been kept prisoners by the savages, who threatened them with death if they tried to move. Padre Fuster sent some of them to look for Padre Jayme, and also sent a messenger to the presidio.

In a little while the mission Indians, wailing aloud, returned with the battered body of their priest, which they laid at Padre Fuster's feet. As he looked at the bloody, beaten body of his brother friar, and saw that only the consecrated hands had been spared the cruel blows, his sobs were added to those of the converts.

A few hours later the Christian Indians bore the priest's body to the presidio. The soldiers were greatly shocked, for they had neither heard the noise of the attack, nor seen the fires of the night before. Captain Ortega was absent, having gone to be present at the founding of San Juan Capistrano Mission.

The next day the burial service was read at the presidio. Now the messenger was ready to go in all haste with Padre Fuster's letter to Rivera, asking for more troops, as another attack might take place at any time.

When the reading of the letter was finished, there was silence for several minutes. Then the captain said, "I return to Monterey tonight, and shall leave with the soldiers as soon as possible."

"And I shall go with you," cried Junípero eagerly, jumping from his chair.

"No, Your Reverence, it is not possible," Rivera told

152

him firmly. We shall travel by forced marches in order to get there as soon as we can. The trip would be much too hard for you. I cannot consent to your going."

The padre did not argue. He merely thought that growing old was a great nuisance. Younger people were always thinking that one was not able to do things which were quite possible. He had a very good reason for wishing to be in San Diego, though, and now he spoke of it to Captain Rivera.

"I hope, sir, that the Indian attackers will not be punished too harshly. They are just simple, ignorant children, who have no idea of how terrible is the crime they have committed. If we show them a spirit of mercy and kindness instead of revenge, they may come to understand how good and charitable is Christ's way, and so, wish to come to His church."

Rivera only looked at the Father President, and made a muffled sound in his throat. Then he bade the padres farewell, and left.

In a few days another messenger arrived with letters from the priests who had gone to found San Juan Capistrano. These messages told how the cross had been set up, work on the buildings begun, two bells hung, and that Sergeant Ortega and his soldier guards had arrived from San Diego. Then the news of the dreadful disaster there had come. Ortega had left at once with part of the guard. The padres had buried the bells, packed the equipment on the mules, and with the remainder of the soldiers, had hurried down to San Diego. So San Juan Capistrano had not been founded, after all. With San Diego gone, there were now only four missions along the road that stretched from San Diego to Monterey.

This was a grave setback and a disappointment, to be sure, but a missionary's life was beset with these. The ways of the Almighty are often hard for mortals to understand. All that could be done was to ask for strength to come through the trials along the way, and to trust that the goal would be reached at last.

What troubled Junípero most at this time was the fear that the Indians at San Diego would be punished so severely that they could consider the white men their enemies. It was not to be expected that their centuries of uncivilized, wild life, which held no idea of right and wrong, could be changed in a few years. Great patience and sympathy were needed, but most of all, the example of kind treatment and forgiveness, to turn them from their savage ways.

The military commander, Junípero knew, did not understand this. If only he could be in San Diego, perhaps he might help Rivera to see that this was the right policy. He longed to go south by himself, but the missionaries were forbidden to travel without a soldier guard for protection. Only the commander could order such a guard. The Father President, therefore, remained at San Carlos, feeling quite helpless. He had to content himself with writing to the Viceroy, urging him to order kind treatment for the Indians, and to hasten the rebuilding of the destroyed mission. It would take months for the letters to reach Mexico City, and a reply to be sent back.

Probably because his heart yearned for the wayward Indians at San Diego, Junípero threw himself, with even more than his usual vigor, into directing the daily life of his own mission at Carmel, where there were now about two hundred fifty people.

He rose at daybreak and had the bells rung for sunrise Mass. As the sweet tones shattered the morning mists, he watched his people pour into the courtyard. The young girls came from the room where they slept. From another building the boys trooped out, as did the Indian families who lived in the grass huts on the mission grounds. The soldiers joined them, and all went into the church.

After Mass the padre went to the kitchen, where great iron kettles were steaming over the fire. They were filled with atole, a kind of mush made of roasted barley, of which the Indians were very fond. He saw to it that the clay or bark bowls were heaped full before they went to the family huts, or the boys' or girls' rooms. Almost always the kitchen was half-full of pagans from nearby villages, to whom Junípero himself handed a brimming bowl. Often he also gave them little gifts of beads or cloth, and asked them to spend the day at the mission.

Breakfast over, the day's work began. The men went to the fields, or to the carpentry or blacksmith shops, or to the forests to bring back wood for fuel. The women went about their tasks of weaving, sewing, or pounding grain. Those who lived in the mission huts were taught how to keep their homes clean and neat. This was very difficult for them, for the California Indians were not naturally given to cleanliness. At this time the young children would gather around the Father President in the reception room for special lessons.

At eleven o'clock the bells called everyone to the noonday meal. Once again the bowls were sent to the kitchen. This time they were filled with pozole, a thick soup made of ground wheat, corn, peas, beans, and sometimes, meat. Then came a time of rest until two in the afternoon, when work was started again.

At about five, as the Angelus sounded, all went to the church again for lessons in the catechism, prayers, and hymns. Supper was an hour later, and consisted of atole, as in the morning. Evening was the time for enjoyment. The Indians danced or played their native games, or held contests, while the padres watched. Bedtime was early so that everyone might get his needed rest before the sunrise rising hour.

As spring came to Carmel, there was great activity in the fields. Larger crops must be planted as more and more people came to live at the mission. This meant clearing more land, plowing, sowing the seeds, watering and weeding the plants. Fray Francisco had taken over the care of the garden. Junípero smiled fondly whenever he looked at it, for it was so much like the good man himself—hardy and useful, but tender and gentle, too. His long, neat rows of beans, lettuce, and cauliflower stood up sturdy and proud. A border of azaleas ran all around the square vegetable bed. The delicate, fluffy, pink and white flowers made a fine contrast to the stout green stalks, heavy with beans.

During his early days at the mission, while he was waiting for the "brown brothers" to come, Junípero had taught himself to sew. He, in turn, had taught the Indian women so that they could make clothes for themselves and their families. The women learned quickly, and some were already teaching the others. The padre still cut out the garments, however, from the huge bolts of cloth the Viceroy had given him.

One spring afternoon, as his scissors were cutting along the outline of a paper pattern for a small child's gown on a length of blue cotton, a chubby five-year-old came close to him. Her big black eyes were pleading silently as she held up a crude doll made of tree bark.

"A gown for the papoose, too? Is that it?" Junípero asked, smiling.

"Yes, old padre," and the dark eyes danced with pleasure.

"Very well, then, she shall have it," he told her.

When the tiny dress had been cut, he sat on a low stool sewing the seams, with the small one at his side. Halfway through, the hand holding the needle rested in his

156

lap, while his eyes traveled through the doorway far out over the western sea. He was seeing, for a moment, another doll lying in a Majorcan courtyard years ago. It was his own sister Juana's doll, much loved because it was "dressed in blue, like our Blessed Lady," as she said. Slowly his eyes returned to the present, while he looked long at the dusky face upturned to his.

For the first time, he thought, he really completely understood Christ's command: "Suffer the little children to come unto Me, and forbid them not, for of such is the Kingdom of Heaven." That kingdom was made up of little brown faces, like the one at his side, as well as white, yellow, and black. How much harder he must try to bring more and more of the brown ones into its holy borders!

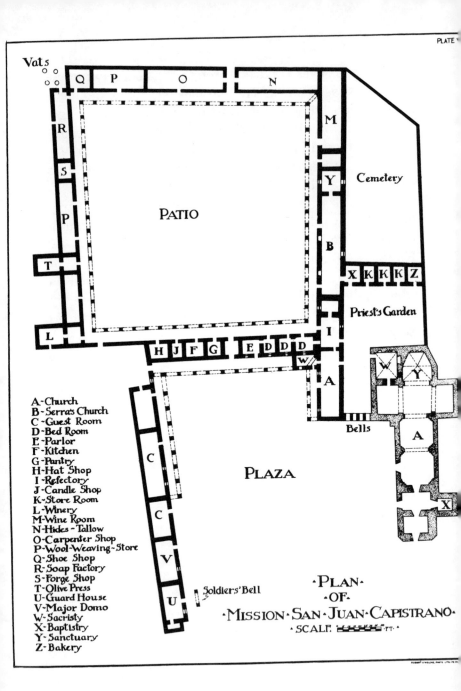

PLATE

Vats

Q P O N M Y Cemetery B X K K K Z Priest's Garden I A Bells

PATIO

R S P T L H J F G E D D D W

A-Church
B-Serra's Church
C-Guest Room
D-Bed Room
E-Parlor
F-Kitchen
G-Pantry
H-Hat Shop
I-Refectory
J-Candle Shop
K-Store Room
L-Winery
M-Wine Room
N-Hides-Tallow
O-Carpenter Shop
P-Wool-Weaving-Store
Q-Shoe Shop
R-Soap Factory
S-Forge Shop
T-Olive Press
U-Guard House
V-Major Domo
W-Sacristy
X-Baptistry
Y-Sanctuary
Z-Bakery

C

C

V

U

PLAZA

W Y A X

Soldiers' Bell

·PLAN·
·OF·
·MISSION·SAN·JUAN·CAPISTRANO·
·SCALE. [scale] FT.·

Courtesy of Bancroft Library.

158

XVIII San Diego Rebuilt— San Juan Capistrano Founded

A gay Spanish song that mingled with the "tlot, lot" of horses' hoofs echoed among the hills and along the little valley at Carmel. It was almost sunset on a March day in 1776. A soldier from Monterey brought the news that Colonel Anza had arrived from Sonora, Mexico, with a company of settlers for the port of Saint Francis.

"There is much bustle and excitement in Monterey this day," the messenger said. "So many people—more than one hundred fifty! And twelve soldiers and their families stayed at San Gabriel, and ten at San Diego in case there should be trouble with the Indians. There are women and little ones! I have not seen a woman of my own race for seven years. It is good to see them in California, at last."

Junípero agreed, and promised to be at the presidio

159

the next day. Early in the morning he, Fray Francisco, and three other missionaries who were at San Carlos, greeted Anza and Padre Font, the Franciscan who had come with the expedition, as well as the settlers. It seemed odd to find the sleepy little presidio alive with activity, and noisy with the babble of Spanish voices. After a Mass of thanksgiving for the safe arrival of the travelers, Anza, Padre Font, and several of the soldiers went, at Junípero's invitation, to stay at the mission. It was a more comfortable place than the barracks.

Though Anza became ill as the result of his hard trip, Padre Serra had many long talks with him. He heard about the journey from Sonora to San Gabriel Mission, lasting ninety-eight days. Due, no doubt, to Anza's care for his people, not one was lost on the way. As a matter of fact, there were more in the group than when it started, for eight babies were born during the journey.

Junípero also heard about affairs at San Diego. Colonel Anza had hurried down there with some of his troops as soon as he had heard the news about the attack from Rivera, who was at San Gabriel on his way south. "I wished to punish the guilty savages thoroughly, and at once, in order to discourage any more outbreaks," the colonel said, "but Rivera only increased their hatred of the white men by dragging out his actions."

"Complete forgiveness would have been better than punishment," the Father President stated. "But tell me what measures have been taken."

"The commander has made raids on the nearby Indian villages, and captured their chiefs to question them about the attack. If the men do not answer his questions, they are severely whipped until they do. If Rivera thinks the chief is guilty, he imprisons him; if not he sets him free. The raids go on for awhile, then stop, then begin again."

"The poor ignorant savages must, indeed, think us

their enemies," declared Junípero, shaking his head.

"Tell me, has the commander begun to rebuild the mission?"

"Nothing has been done in that matter, at all," Anza reported. "Frankly, Your Reverence, I was glad to receive word from San Gabriel that their food supplies would not last if my people stayed much longer. It was a relief to get away from San Diego. I left ten soldiers there, and went at once to join the colonists for the final stage of our journey. Before I left, Rivera promised that the mission and fort at the port of Saint Francis would not be delayed more than two months."

"Thank God for that," said Junípero warmly.

However, while Anza still lay ill at Carmel, a messenger arrived with a letter from Commander Rivera saying that the colony on San Francisco Bay could not be started for a year or more. He did not explain why.

Anza, nevertheless, took a party to explore the region, hoping that on his return he would find a letter giving permission to begin the settlement much sooner. No such message came, and Anza set out for the south.

Once more Junípero felt that the work of saving souls in California was going to be held back by a military commander who was overcome by his own power, and not willing to work with the missionaries. When the Viceroy had recalled Fages, the padre thought such troubles were over. Rivera, in his way, was proving to be just as troublesome. Now, no progress was being made. In fact, it seemed as if they were going backward, instead of ahead. Through it all, he must stay in Carmel, helpless to change the course of events.

To his great surprise, he soon received word that Rivera was in Monterey, and wished to see him, but was unable to come to Carmel because of illness. When the Father President arrived in Monterey, he found that the illness was only a pain in one leg. It was clear that something pressed heavily on the Commander's mind, but Junípero was not prepared for what came from the Captain's lips.

"I have come to you as Father President for absolution," he said. "Padre Fuster of San Diego has excommunicated me."

"What?" cried Junípero, unbelievingly. "What was the reason?"

In answer, Rivera handed him a letter from Padre Fuster and the other missionaries, while he gave a brief account of what had taken place. The letters had been opened, Junípero noticed, but the captain said it had been done by accident.

"This is a very serious matter," the Father President told Rivera, "and I must have the opinion of the other friars. I shall let you know what is decided."

Back in Carmel with Padres Palou, Crespi, and the three other missionaries about him, Junípero read of the happenings that had led to Padre Fuster's action.

Carlos, one of the converts at San Diego, had taken part in the attack on the mission. He came back, seeming to be sorry for his deed, and took refuge in the building that was being used for a chapel. He knew that the rule of the Church, coming down from the time of Moses, was that he could not be taken from the church by officers unless they agreed in writing to give him a fair trial. When Rivera was told that the Indian was there, he ordered Padre Fuster to turn him over, as the building was really only a warehouse, and not a church. The padre replied that he could not give the man up, since the right of refuge applied to any place where Holy Mass was celebrated. He further told the commander that anyone who took Carlos by force would be excommunicating himself. Rivera paid no attention to this warning, and,

162

with drawn sword, went in himself, and dragged the Indian out. The wayward convert was then taken to the guardhouse, and put into the stocks. At this point, Padre Fuster announced the order of excommunication.

Far into the night the six Franciscans at Carmel discussed the matter, and asked God to guide them in making the right decision. Finally, they all agreed that Padre Fuster's action was correct. The Father President sent this word to Rivera, but pointed out that if the Indian, Carlos, were taken back to the chapel, and put under the missionaries' charge, Rivera could receive absolution.

Rivera was returning to San Diego, of course, and once more Junípero asked to be allowed to go with him, and the captain again refused, as might have been expected.

The spring days, which brought blue skies above and a fragrant carpet of wild flowers to the hillsides, wore on, but the Father President's heart was heavy with the thought that no progress was being made. Then, one day late in June, the sails of the *San Antonio*, rising and falling, as the good ship rode into the bay, once more brought a ray of hope. Hurrying over to Monterey, he learned that the ship was going back down the coast to San Diego. Here was the chance he had been praying for! When she sailed south, he was determined to be on board.

In the meantime, Rivera had sent an order giving permission to start the presidio at the port of Saint Francis, but again postponing the founding of the mission there. However, when the party of soldiers and their families under Lieutenant Moraga, who had come with Anza, set out, Junípero saw to it that Padre Palou went along. Thus, he would be on the spot in case the order to begin the mission should be given.

As Junípero went aboard the *San Antonio*, his thoughts were on the man from his native island of Majorca, who had been the ship's captain for so long. After leaving

Monterey, Juan Pérez had died at sea after his second voyage to the northwest coast. The padre realized now how great a friend he had lost. He was soon to find that he had gained a new friend, though, in the new captain, Don Diego Choquet.

After a voyage of twelve days, the Father President arrived to find San Diego a place of utter idleness. The soldiers at the presidio lolled in front of their barracks, or sat talking in little groups beneath the trees, while those on guard duty rested on their muskets. Padre Fuster and the two missionaries assigned to San Juan Capistrano had had nothing to do for eight months. They were very depressed, and begged to be sent back to Mexico. Even Rivera had stopped his raids on the Indian villages, and had quit punishing the savages, who seemed to have no idea of again attacking the Spaniards. Yet, in spite of all this, not a move had been made to begin rebuilding the ruined mission.

Junípero, true to his nature, resolved to do something about this state of affairs. The well of energy that had made it possible for him to do unbelievable things in the past, still inhabited his frail, aging form, and was far from running dry. It gushed forth now with all its old power and vigor.

Knowing that the *San Antonio* was to remain in port until the middle of October, he decided to ask the captain for help. "Sir," he said to Don Diego Choquet, "it must pain you, as it does me, to see the mission of your patron saint, San Diego, in ruins. Would you permit your sailors to help in the work of restoring it while the ship is in port?"

"With much pleasure," the good captain replied at once. "Not only the sailors, but I myself will labor as a common workman at whatever needs to be done."

"God will reward both you and your crew," the padre

replied. "I shall ask the commander to furnish us a soldier guard, and we shall begin at once."

In the heat of late summer, the group of twenty armed sailors with two of their officers, as well as some twenty or more Indian converts, and the soldier guard, followed the Father President, two of the missionaries, and Captain Choquet up the river to the site of the destroyed mission. At once they all set to work. Stones were carried, holes dug for the foundations, adobe bricks made. Two weeks passed, and it looked as if the adobe wall, which was to enclose the square, would be built within a fortnight. Then, at the rate the work was going, all the buildings might be completed before the *San Antonio* left.

One day Junípero found it necessary to go to the presidio. He seemed to be walking on air as he reflected that he had never known more willing workers, nor seen plans carried out more speedily. Soon California's first mission would be ready once more to bring hope and comfort to the *Gentiles* of San Diego, he thought.

His lightness of heart did not last long, though. On his return, he was met by the downcast faces of the friars and the captain. Junípero looked from one to another, and urged them to speak.

"Commander Rivera has been here," Captain Choquet told him, at last. "He has ordered the guard back to the presidio, and told me to withdraw my men."

"But why?" cried the Father President.

"He said he had heard from one of the converts that the Indians were preparing arrows for another attack. I reminded him that there had been such a story going about once before, but it had been false. When I asked him if he had tried to find out the truth of this rumor, he said he had not, but as all the Indians were talking about it, it must be so. Then I told him that it would be better to send a larger guard here than to withdraw, and bring shame to our Spanish soldiers. This made him very angry, and he left with orders to the guard to retire to the presidio. I feel that with all our armed men here, there is no reason to go. However, I do not wish to quarrel with Rivera, so I suppose we must."

Junípero looked at the piles of stones and adobes, at the unfinished wall. His dream of the new mission crashed about him with a thud. Quietly he said, "Let the Will of God be done, for He alone can provide the remedy."

Junípero was convinced that when the Viceroy had received his reports, as well as those of Anza and Captain Choquet, his excellency would send orders reversing Rivera's decisions. He could only wait in San Diego for them to arrive.

One day, a little more than two weeks after the work on the mission had been stopped, an Indian from Lower California appeared. "Spanish soldiers are coming," he announced at the presidio. "There are twenty-five of them, in charge of a corporal. They will be here in a few days now."

They are being sent to add to our forces here at the presidio, I am sure," Rivera said hopefully.

Junípero was hopeful, too, but his hope was that they were guards for the new missions. Indeed, if they were not, the future of his plans looked dark, for the military commander seemed determined to prevent the rebuilding of San Diego, and founding of the others.

As the days passed, Junípero watched the road from the south, torn between hope and fear. He was reminded of the days, years before, when he had watched the sea for the *San Antonio*, which would mean that California was not to be abandoned, after all. Then, just as the blessed sight of the sails had come to him out of the fog, a messenger came riding one evening with a letter from the Viceroy. The soldiers were to guard the missions!

166

The next day, dirty and weary, the men marched into the presidio. Their corporal at once handed the Father President another message from the Viceroy. As he read it, a glow of happiness erased the lines of doubt from his face.

"Set the bells to ringing!" he cried. "The work of saving souls in California is to go on."

As the joyful tones rolled out over the brown hillsides and the lazy blue waters, he read the letter to his brother friars. It stated that orders had been sent to Commander Rivera that San Diego Mission was to be rebuilt at once, and San Juan Capistrano founded. Moreover, the leaders of the attack on the mission were not to be punished, but forgiven, as Junípero had wished. The Viceroy seemed to think that the two missions near San Francisco Bay had already been started, and permission was given for founding those at Santa Bárbara. In addition, the letter said that Rivera was to be recalled, and that the Governor of California, Don Felipe Neve, would move to Monterey.

Actually, there had been a major reorganization in the system of government for the outlying provinces. By royal order, Lower California and Upper California had been placed under one jurisdiction late in 1776, with a Commandant General at its head. Teodoro de Croix, nephew of the former Viceroy, became the first Commandant, with his capital at the small town of Arispe, Sonora, Mexico. This meant that Bucareli, always a good friend of the Father President and his program, would no longer have direct control over the missions.

When this realization became clear, a momentary chill of apprehension swept over Junípero as the unknown future loomed before him. That was something to be dealt with later, however. For the present, he rejoiced in this latest evidence of Viceroy Bucareli's coöperation.

167

"Tomorrow," Padre Serra said, as the notes of the bells died away, "we shall sing a High Mass of thanksgiving, and then I shall write the good Viceroy a letter of hearty thanks."

The missionaries, of course, were overjoyed. Not so Rivera, who now had to reverse his own orders, release his prisoners, and assign the mission guards he had refused before. As soon as possible, he fled to Monterey.

The work began where it had stopped at the old mission site up the river from the presidio. It went so well that in a few weeks Junípero felt he could leave for San Juan Capistrano.

With the two friars who were to remain at the new mission, a guard of eleven soldiers, and the pack animals well laden with equipment, the Father President started. October, with her golden days of soft, clear sunshine, was drawing to a close, but summer lingered along the California coast over which they trudged between the oldest mission and this newest one. Always in sight on the left was the blue Pacific, lapping softly on pale beaches, or crashing with flung spray against a rocky shore. On the right stretched the mountains, whose jagged tops caught the rosy tints of dawn and the purple shadows of twilight. Some fifty miles from their starting point, Padre Serra led the little party off the trail into a lovely valley, where Portolá had camped on his trip in search of Monterey. There were broad pastures all about, and so many wild grapevines that the land looked like a vineyard. The cross that Padre Lasuén had set up on a slight rise of ground was still standing near the little river that hurried down to the sea.

Digging for the buried bells began at once. When they were brought forth and hung from a tree, their joyful notes called to the Indian villages nearby. The savages came in great numbers, smiling and happy that the padres had returned. The usual shelter of boughs was made for the altar, where the first Mass was said on November 1st, 1776, and Mission San Juan Capistrano was founded.

The Father President was so eager to get the mission started at once, that he made a trip to San Gabriel to bring back some converts to help with the buildings. He also brought supplies, and the cattle which had been left there.

On the return trip, it seemed to Junípero that he could not wait to get to the new mission. Yet the cattle and the pack animals moved so slowly that they seemed to be standing still. Speaking to one of the converts and a soldier who had been walking beside him, the padre said, "Come, let us go on a little ahead. This pace is too slow for me."

When the three were about halfway to the mission, a crowd of yelling, painted savages suddenly sprang out in front of them, fixing their arrows to the bows, ready to kill them. Junípero stood quite still in the dusty road. Once again he looked squarely into the face of death— a martyr's death—as he had several times before in his life; once again it was snatched from him, though he would have welcomed it as a fitting end to his labors. The Indian convert shouted to the attackers, saying that they should not harm the padre, as there were many soldiers coming, who would kill them all. Stunned at hearing their own language, they dropped their bows. Junípero urged them to come nearer, while he made the sign of the cross on the forehead of each one. Then, reaching down into the huge pockets of his robe, he drew out beads of red, yellow, and blue, which he placed in the hands of the delighted pagans, who had, by this time, become quite friendly.

With the help which had been brought from San Gabriel,

the work on the buildings went ahead rapidly. Before long, the Father President decided to leave it in the hands of the other two missionaries, and return to Carmel.

On the way he stopped at San Gabriel, San Luis Obispo, and San Antonio, bringing to the converts his blessing and fatherly love, and to the missionaries, encouragement in their hardships, and praise for work well done. At each mission he stopped long enough to baptize some of the Indians. "Now," he said, "I am, indeed, a father to all the missions, for I have spiritual children in each of them."

XIX Santa Clara and San Francisco de Asisi

"Has the mission of our father, Saint Francis, been founded yet?" Junípero asked as soon as the gates of San Carlos closed behind him, and he had greeted Fray Juan Crespi. He had heard no word about this while in the south.

"He has both a mission and a presidio at his port," Fray Juan answered, "and the Mission of Santa Clara, between here and San Francisco, was started this very month of January, 1777."

"God be thanked," exclaimed the Father President. "I must go at once to see them."

He was detained in Carmel, though, by the news that the new Governor, Don Felipe de Neve, was arriving shortly to make his headquarters in Monterey.

Early in February the guns of the presidio, booming

their salute, announced the Governor's appearance. His only communication from the official since he had taken command, was a request for inventories of all the missions. Since the Father President had been sending in such reports in duplicate to the College of San Fernando —one to be sent on to the Viceroy—for the last four years, he had merely informed Neve of this fact.

Had he known that the new Governor had considered this a defiance of his orders, and an attempt at concealment of the true state of the missions, Junípero would have really dreaded the impending meeting. He only knew that Neve had quarreled with the Dominican friars in Lower California. What if he disliked missionaries in general, and would try to work against them at every turn, as it seemed to him that Fages and Rivera had done? The Father President decided to lay his plans for the future of the missions before Governor Neve, and to get his reaction without delay.

The first meeting went well. Junípero spoke of his wish to found San Buenaventura, so long delayed, in the Santa Bárbara region. Besides this, there should be at least two more in that vicinity, he told the Governor, to form a link between the northern and southern missions. Without such a link, hostile Indians might be able to break the line of communication. Neve seemed much impressed with the plans, and agreed that three missions and a presidio, as well, should be built there.

This appeared to be a favorable beginning, and Junípero felt cheered about the future. He could take time now to visit the two new missions he had not seen. Eagerly he set out on foot, and after a few days came to a great plain, dotted with clumps of giant oak trees, and many Indian villages.

His steps finally brought him to Santa Clara, set in meadowland near a grove of laurels on the River Guada-

172

A pastoral scene at Mission Santa Clara, founded January 12, 1777.

lupe. It was still just a shelter of poles and boughs, but a new church of wood, plastered with clay, had been started. Padre Murguía knew something of architecture, and he was busy directing the few soldiers and three Indians in constructing the buildings he had planned. Ditches were also being dug to bring water from the river for the crops.

The Father President had not sent word that he was coming. Hence, the two Franciscans were greatly surprised and very happy to see him.

"Tell me about your first days here," Junípero begged.

"I arrived here with Lietenant Moraga, nine soldiers with their families, and one family of settlers early in January," Padre de la Peña began. "The cross was set up, a shelter built, and I said the first Mass here on January 12th. Then we cleared a square of two hundred feet for the buildings. Padre Murguía arrived from Carmel with the mission goods, equipment, and cattle about ten days later."

173

"Did the *Gentiles* come to you freely?" asked the Father President, always more interested in his "brown brothers" than in all else.

"Yes, they came," put in Padre Murguía wryly, "but only to steal our cattle. Cow after cow disappeared. Finally, some of the thieves were caught and punished. We hated to do this so soon after our arrival, but our herd was fast disappearing."

"Were the Indians unfriendly because of it?" asked Junípero.

"Yes. It was very discouraging at first. We had no baptisms, and the pagans would not come to the mission. Then something happened that changed the situation."

"What was that?"

"A great sickness came upon the people. The children, especially, were affected, and many died. Padre de la Peña and I started going about the villages, asking to baptize the sick children. On June 6th the first Indian baby received the Sacrament. From that time on, the people have been friendly."

"May they continue so," was Junípero's wish, "and repay your work here with many converts."

After saying Mass at the new mission, and resting for a day, he set out once more. His heart swelled with the thought that at his journey's end he would see for himself the mighty port his father, Saint Francis, had, indeed, shown to his followers. The trail was newly-made, and rough. It ambled through the wide plain, past an ancient redwood tree that towered above the highest oaks, and through rushing creeks. Though his lame leg was paining badly, the old padre would not stop, for ahead of him were his newest mission, San Francisco de Asís, and his oldest friend, Fray Francisco Palou. The night was half spent, and some forty-five miles had been traveled that day, when, near the foot of two matching peaks, on a sparkling lagoon, he saw a little cluster of huts. So weary was he that he almost fell into the arms of the astonished, but delighted, Fray Francisco.

"I have come to be with you for the feast day of our holy father, Saint Francis," he announced simply.

Three days later, on the feast day, October 4th, the troops and colonists came over from the presidio. With the seventeen Indians who had been converted, they heard High Mass sung by the Father President, and the special sermon he preached on the life of the "little poor man of Assisi."

In the meantime he had heard from Fray Francisco the story of the founding of the mission. "As you know, Padre, our expedition under Lieutenant Moraga left Monterey on June 17th of last year. We came by the route you traveled, but because of the large families of the colonists, we went very slowly. The Indians we met were friendly, but amazed at our cattle, for they had never seen such animals before."

"Yes, the cow was unknown in California before we came, it seems," Junípero put in.

"We also saw some animals unknown to us. On the wide plain you crossed in coming here, we saw a herd of what looked like large deer with huge spreading antlers. The soldiers killed three of them, and the meat which was very good, lasted for several days. Besides these animals, which are called elk, we also saw herds of deer and antelope."

"The deer and antelope we have all seen to the southward, but the elk is an animal new to me," Junípero told him.

"After ten days of traveling, we came to this lagoon, which empties into an arm of the sea. At that time of year its shores were bordered with hundreds of blue lilies. Colonel Anza had named it 'Laguna de las Dolores' for

Our Lady of Sorrows. Here we pitched fifteen tents, and made camp. A shelter of boughs was built, and the next day I said Mass. All stayed here a month waiting for the *San Carlos* to come into port."

"The ship was delayed?"

"Yes. It was nearly two months before it came, having been driven far southward by the strong winds. Lieutenant Moraga had already moved on with most of the soldiers and colonists to a place near the entrance of the port. Much timber had been cut. With the help of the sailors from the *San Carlos*, the buildings for the presidio were built, as well as these at the mission. Formal possession of the presidio in the name of our King took place on September 17th after Holy Mass and the singing of the 'Te Deum'. Then the cannon on ship and shore boomed out, echoed by the muskets of the soldiers."

"And the mission?" Junípero wanted to know.

"We waited and waited for permission for the founding to come from Commander Rivera. Meanwhile, the officers from the ship and the presidio explored this huge port and the surrounding land. They found that we are on a peninsula, with water on three sides, and the only gateway to the sea in front of us. The port itself consists of three large bays, or arms of the ocean, with several rivers emptying into them."

Junípero smiled. "Our spiritual father, Saint Francis, had given us a real port!"

"It must be among the best anywhere in the world," Fray Francisco said. "When the exploring party returned," he continued, "a conference was held, and it was decided to found the mission, even though no word had come from Rivera. It was time for the *San Carlos* to leave, and Captain Quirós wanted to give a report to the Viceroy of all that had taken place. Besides, we had enough soldiers to act as guards."

"I think you were right in doing so," he was assured.

"When Rivera visited here last year, he told us that he was pleased with what had been done," Francisco said. He continued, "On October 8th then, the cross was set up and blessed, and a procession held in honor of Saint Francis, with an image of him carried on a platform, and later placed on the altar. The church had been decorated with flags, pennants, and bunting from the *San Carlos*. Firecrackers and rockets were set off, while the soldiers fired their muskets, and the sailors discharged a small cannon brought from the ship. Later all the people remained for a feast, for which we killed two beeves. It was a happy day on which we gave our whole-hearted devotion to Saint Francis.

"May the saintly founder of our order be with you here in all you do, Fray Francisco," said the Father President with meaning. Then he went on, "We have not spoken of the *Gentiles* of this region. Have they been friendly?"

"As soon as we made a camp here, many of them came to see us, making signs of pleasure and friendship at our being here. They seemed pleased with our gifts, which they returned in the form of shell-fish and grass seeds. While we were waiting for the ship to come, the padres and I visited their villages, and we were always well received. They returned the visits with courtesy, whole villages of the pagans coming to see us with their little gifts."

"Not many have come to be baptised, though?" Junípero asked.

"For about eight months there were no Indians here, at all," Fray Francisco told him. "Their enemies, from about eighteen miles to the southeast, had begun to make war on them, burning their villages, and injuring many. We knew nothing about it until nearly all had fled in their rush canoes to islands in the bay, or to other shores. They left the month before the mission was formally founded, and did not begin to return until March of this year. Slowly they have begun coming to us, and our first baptisms were in August on Saint John the Baptist's Day. More and more are coming now since they are over their fear of their enemies."

"Your mission will prosper, I know," Padre Serra told him. "Our holy father, Saint Francis, was the greatest missionary of all. He will not ignore the work of his own mission."

One day while he was at Mission Dolores, Junípero went with Fray Francisco to see the presidio and the harbor. The two old padres stood on a headland above the gateway leading from the ocean to the bay. Junípero's whole being thrilled to the magnificent scene. Shading his eyes with his hand, he looked to the right across the great bay to its eastern coast. In front was the narrow entrance from the sea with a wooded strand directly opposite. To the left across the wavy sand dunes, the waters of the mighty Pacific stretched on and on to wash countless unknown shores.

"Thanks be to God!" the Father President exclaimed. "Our father, Saint Francis, with the holy cross· of the mission procession, has reached the end of the continent; to go on, he must have boats."

His mind flashed back to the day when, as a child, he had carried the cross at the head of the procession for his friend, Pedro. That was more than a half century before, yet for most of those years he had carried the cross, as a missionary, to the heathen peoples of the New World. As he stood on the rocky height, with the brisk, cool wind from the Pacific blowing his robes, and rumpling his gray Franciscan fringe of hair, he bowed his head, and murmured: "The blessed cross, O Lord—it was the burden I have most wished to carry in this life."

"It has come! It has come!" Junípero shouted to Juan Crespi, as he waved a paper in his hand.

"What has come, Fray Junípero?" the other asked, entering the mission office at Carmel.

"My permit to administer the Sacrament of Confirmation," Junípero replied joyfully.

He had just received the mail which had been brought down by messenger, who also brought a beautiful altar vessel for San Carlos as a parting gift from Bucareli.

"It is well that we have been teaching our converts so that they are ready to be confirmed," said Fray Juan.

"Yes. Now, thanks be to God, our 'brown brothers' can become full members of our Holy Church. We must send word at once to all the missions."

Usually, only a bishop has the right to give Confirmation. However, when Padre Serra had first gone to Lower

179

California, he had asked permission from the Pope for himself, or some other priest, to give the Sacrament, as it seemed unlikely that a bishop would ever come to California. The permit had been granted, but it had to be approved by so many officials, that it had taken four years for it to arrive. As it was to last for ten years, only six years now remained.

"We must make haste, Fray, so that as many as possible can be taken into the fold before the permit expires," Junípero urged, his tired old eyes aglow with the light that had led him ever onward in his crusade to Christianize the Indians.

In less than two weeks, ninety-one children at Carmel were given the Sacrament that was to make them "strong and perfect Christians, and soldiers of Jesus Christ." Then the adults, some Spaniards who had not been confirmed in childhood, as well as Indian converts, were given lessons. Within two months, all were ready to receive the Sacrament.

The *Santiago* now prepared to sail south from Monterey, and the Father President went with her to San Diego.

After giving the Sacrament at the southern mission, he once again made the long hard trip on foot from San Diego to Carmel, stopping at each mission along the way. At the end of the journey, in January of the year 1779, his Book of Confirmations contained the names of one thousand eight hundred ninety-seven persons.

The last steps of the incredible trip of more than four hundred miles were the most painful he had ever taken, for his foot and leg were so badly inflamed that he could hardly walk. How good it was to see the bent old cypresses along the shore, and to hear the wind singing in the pines once more as he hobbled along. The sights and sounds meant that he was nearing that beloved spot which was home to him. The gray fog that closed in on

Carmel soon after his arrival seemed like soft, silvery wings folding him to rest after his wearying journey.

Yes, it was good to be home again in his own mission with the faithful Juan Crespi and his mission Indians, but he longed to go to the two northern missions to confirm there. The bad state of his leg made this impossible for many months, however. Meanwhile, there were signs that the new Governor did not mean to work in sympathy with the Franciscans.

Once again a request had come from the Governor for information about the missions. With the request were special inventory and census forms drawn up by Neve himself.

"Fray Juan," Junípero remarked when he saw them, "our Governor seems determined to take our time and tax our patience with demands for these mission inventories. Surely he must know that our only duty in these matters is to our Franciscan superiors, not to the civil authorities."

"Yes, Fray Junípero. Perhaps you should remind him that your reports are sent regularly to the College of San Fernando, and go on to the Viceroy."

Accordingly, the Father President wrote to Neve that his report would be sent "directly." The Governor, though, interpreted this word as meaning "soon" (which it does, also, of course—in Spanish as well as English), and he was extremely perturbed when it did not arrive, at all, for he was under orders from de Croix to obtain the inventories. What, he wondered, were the missionaries trying to conceal?

On the afternoon of Palm Sunday in 1779, Junípero sat at his desk. He would write for a time, read his letter over, frown, tear it up, and start again. This continued until late at night, when he decided to postpone the letter until morning. He was trying to decide what to write to

Governor Neve about the demand he had made for the election of alcaldes by the converts. The alcalde was to be a sort of mayor and justice of the peace combined. Neve insisted that the Indians of the missions be allowed to select alcaldes from their own number, so that they might become used to governing themselves.

That morning Junípero had gone to the presidio at Monterey to say Mass. He had arrived early, and the governor had come to talk with him.

"Your Reverence is aware of my wish to have the mission Indians elect their alcaldes. I desire that the elections be held without delay at all the missions."

At these words, the friar felt a storm of turmoil rising within him. Criticism of the missionaries' manner of treating the Indians was almost more than he could bear. He answered calmly, though. "Your honor knows the feeling of the missionaries on the matter. We know that the Indians here are not ready to take this step. It is true that the alcalde system has been used for some time in Mexico. There the Indians are much more civilized, and had had forms of government among their tribes before the Conquest. Then, too, most of those converts had lived in the missions for a long time. Most of our Indians have been with us for a very short time. They are only children, not capable of taking any responsibility."

"They will always be children if you padres continue to treat them as such. They must become used to governing themselves. As you know, Your Reverence, it was always intended that the missions would become little towns, with the padres acting as the village priests. The Indians must be prepared for the time when this comes to pass."

Junípero clenched his cold hands. "We padres, who have lived with the natives day in and day out, know

182

them much better than anyone else. We know that they must be guided and trained for a long time yet," he answered.

"Yes, the missionaries would like to have the Indians in their power forever, I suppose," the governor rejoined. "The welfare of the natives demands that they be allowed to develop themselves."

Junípero's face grew ashen as he demanded in a calm voice, "Do you think that the missionaries are not interested in their welfare, Your Honor? Is it not for this alone that we came to these shores, and have toiled without ceasing for all the years that we have been here?"

"Yes, yes, I know," Neve replied hastily. "You have done much for them in the past. Now this new plan must be put into effect. I shall expect to hear in a few days how the elections are to be carried out."

The governor was gone, and Junípero had to try to compose himself before approaching the altar. The rest of the day he was in distress, trying to decide what he should do. It was after midnight when he gave up his letter writing, and retired to his room to lie down. Through his unsettled thoughts he seemed to sense a voice speaking to him.

"What is it, Lord?" he cried out.

From somewhere within him came the answer, "Wise as the serpents, and simple as the doves."

He sat up with relief, and said, "Yes, Lord, so shall it be, with Thy Grace," and at once was asleep.

Next morning he saw very clearly how the matter could be arranged. The governor's orders would be carried out, but the candidates would be those Indians who were already police officers. They wore a special suit, and carried a baton. If they became alcaldes, the people would not be aware that a few of them had been given unusual power. The greatest trouble would arise from the fact that the alcaldes were not to be punished for wrongdoing. Junípero knew that this would be very bad for keeping order in the missions, but he saw no way to avoid it.

He wrote the Governor, then, that the elections would be carried out. The system, even according to Junípero's plan, did not work out well, though. The alcaldes, knowing they could not be physically punished, were guilty of all sorts of crimes, and the mission rule suffered much.

In time, Neve recognized its failure, and made no effort to enforce the alcalde system. Eventually, it simply died out.

This was the fate, too, of the Governor's scheme to transform the missions into villages at once, by refusing to use the term "mission," and substituting for it the word "parish." When he had first spoken to Junípero about this in the year after his arrival at Monterey, the padre had replied, "For the past thirty years I have known the difference between a mission in a heathen country and a parish in a Christian land. If our missions are not missions, then there are none, and there never will be one upon the earth."

The officers and soldiers continued to speak of the "missions," as they had always done, and even de Croix himself used the term in a letter to the Father President. Junípero, of course, was quick to point this out to Neve, who then gave up his attempt to change the established terminology.

One of Neve's regulations in his design to bring the mission system under state control stated that the Governor must approve the appointment and retirement of all priests of mission posts in California. In practice, this was a purely routine matter of sanctioning what had already been done by San Fernando, and Neve knew that if he attempted to intervene between the Father President and his College of San Fernando, that Padre Serra would make good his threat to return at once to Mexico.

Another directive stipulated that there should be no more than one missionary at each mission establishment. Aside from the fact that one man could not possibly oversee the activities of the larger missions, there was no shortage of priests, for there were several in California awaiting future assignments. Also, their expenses were not paid by the government. But this regulation played a very discordant note on the heartstrings of the compassionate Junípero.

His mind's eye flashed down the long corridor of the years to the lonely mission of Santa Gertrudis, perched on a rocky ledge overlooking a desolate chasm in Lower California. He saw the shuddering young missionary assigned there, sitting with his hands covering his face. Behind them were loneliness-haunted eyes tinged with the wild stare that could portend future insanity.

Unable, also, to forget the devastating effect that enforced solitude had on his own spirit, he wrote at once to San Fernando to ask the King's intervention. In the course of time, a royal message prohibited the carrying out of this decree.

Early in October he said to Juan Crespi, "More than a year has passed since I received the permit to confirm, and I have not been to the missions of Santa Clara and San Francisco.

Also, I wish to speak to the missionaries in person about the ruling by the Commandant General that the order for their double rations is stopped, but they need not repay for those already used."

"That, at least, is a blessing," replied Fray Juan, "but doesn't Don Teodoro know that new missions must have food to attract the Indians to come to them, and later on to feed them?"

"It is my belief that the Commandant General, who

has never been in California, and knows little about conditions here, does whatever Felipe de Neve asks him to do," answered Junípero.

Rivera had made the ruling that the priests at all existing missions and those waiting in California for their missions to be established, should have double rations for five years. Neve, soon after his arrival, had ordered them discontinued for San Francisco, Santa Clara, and San Juan Capistrano, which had not yet been founded. The missionaries for these stations were already there, however. He had further ordered that the priests should make restitution to the government for supplies already used. This was almost impossible to do, of course, and the Father President had appealed to de Croix.

Junípero shook his head in response to Padre Crespi's question. "Sometimes it seems," he said musingly, "as if the present government does not wish to see the mission project succeed. At any rate, I have decided to delay no longer in going to Santa Clara and San Francisco."

"Then you will go on muleback, of course," Fray Juan said. "You cannot possibly walk with your leg and foot in such terrible condition."

"No, Fray, I shall walk, as usual."

"But it is impossible, Padre. You will fall along the way, and not be able to go on."

"It is a journey I must make, for the Lord's sake; therefore He will give me strength to do it."

So, in spite of his brother Franciscan's pleading, he started out. Every step was an agony, and when he had gone the eighty miles to Santa Clara, he was so weary that he could barely stand. As he approached the mission gates from the south, he saw a cloud of dust on the trail to the north. "Other travelers are coming to Santa Clara, too," he said to his soldier guards.

What a wonderful surprise was in store for the exhausted padre! The other travelers were Francisco Palou with the captains of the two ships that had returned from exploring the northern coast. They were on their way to Carmel with the ship's doctor to treat the Father President's foot. As usual, he put off applying the remedies the doctor offered, though.

"You are most kind, my friends, but I think it would be better to wait until we have reached San Francisco. The remedy might make the sore worse for a time, and so I would not be able to make the journey, at all."

When San Francisco was reached, and he had rested a bit, he told the doctor that he felt better. Besides, it would require a long treatment, he said, for he had had it for many years. Since he could stay only a few days, such treatment would be useless. "It would really be better to leave it in the hands of the Divine Physician," he told the doctor. So it was that he left his bodily malady in the hands of God, as he did all else in life.

When he had been with Fray Francisco some days, giving the Sacrament to all who were prepared to receive it, a messenger arrived from Lower California. He brought news of the death of Viceroy Bucareli, and of the outbreak of war between Spain and England. No one was much concerned about the war, for California was too far away. Junípero felt, though, that the death of his good friend was a great blow to the missions. He was anxious about the future.

"We can only trust in God," he said to Francisco Palou, as he took his leave of San Francisco's Mission Dolores, "in whose name all our work has been done."

On his return trip he stopped not only at Santa Clara, but at the pueblo of San Jose. This, the first Spanish town in California, had been founded by Lieutenant Moraga two years before, with sixty-six colonists from Anza's expedition.

Leaving Santa Clara Mission, Junípero traveled about two miles to the south, and crossed the Guadalupe River, swollen by early fall rains. He remembered that Fray Francisco had told him of eating delicious large trout that had come from that stream in the summer.

As he approached the plaza, or central square, of the pueblo, the alcalde came out to meet him. The official pointed out the fourteen houses of plastered wood, one for each family, all set in their own ample plots of land. Each family had its own fields for wheat, corn, beans, and other vegetables, too. Beyond, were pastures for their cattle, sheep, goats, and horses.

"Are you well satisfied with your life here?" Junípero asked the alcalde.

"Oh yes, Padre. We had a good harvest this year, and even had a little more than we needed for our own use. This we sold to the soldiers. Next year we hope to plant more, and have more to sell."

A few days after Junípero's return to his own mission, Governor Neve dismounted from his horse, and strode into the mission office. The padre's worst fears about Felipe de Neve as Governor were about to be realized.

"You have been giving the Sacrament of Confirmation in your missions, is it not so?"

"Why, yes, sir, ever since I received the permit to do so more than a year ago."

"Had the permit been signed by the Commandant General?" Neve asked.

"It was signed by the Council of the Indies, and by Viceroy Bucareli," the Father President answered. "I can show you a letter from His Excelency, the Viceroy, congratulating me on having been granted this right, and for confirming so many in the past year."

Padre Serra brought the letter from his desk, and handed it to his visitor. Neve glanced through it. Tapping the paper with his fingers, he said, "This is not good any longer. The office of the Viceroy does not have direct control over California. Commandant de Croix is the head now, and I am his representative."

"Well, then, it will be an easy matter for you to affix your signature," and Junípero reached for his quill.

"The signature would have to be on the original permit," Neve countered. "Do you have it here?"

"Oh no, sir. It is at the College of San Fernando in Mexico City."

"Then, until you can show me the original papers, and I have orders from the Commandant General, you will stop administering Confirmation." The Governor of California turned on his heel, and left.

Junípero stared at Neve's back in disbelief. Was it possible that the Governor would go to such lengths to show his dislike for the missionaries, and his own desire for power?

Fray Juan was outraged when he heard the news. "But this is a religious matter, Fray Junípero. The Governor has no right to withdraw your permit to give the Sacrament. That is for the church officials to decide, not the civil authorities."

"Yes, I know."

"Why didn't you refuse to accept his orders?" Juan wanted to know.

"I have to think what is best for the future of the missions," Junípero replied. "An open quarrel with the Governor would get me nowhere. He will be forced to reinstate the permit when the papers are sent from San Fernando. If he is opposed now, he might refuse even to let us continue to baptize."

"Perhaps you are right, Padre, but I cannot understand how an official of the royal government can withdraw a right which only the church can give," Fray

Juan said.

"For the present, at least, I shall let matters rest," Junípero said, "after I have written San Fernando. We can only trust that God, in His own good time, will set things right."

Suddenly, he realized that he was old and very tired—almost too tired to go on. Still, he must, for the welfare of his "brown brothers." He bowed his head, and resolved to submit to this humiliation with patience. Until the papers came from San Fernando, he would not visit the other missions. The Indians would wonder why he was not conferring Confirmation. They could never understand why Neve would have the power to give orders to their Father President. The influence of the missions, in general, might be destroyed. No, he would remain at Carmel until the Governor restored his right to confirm.

It was easy enough to decide to postpone confirming, but the time came when he had to make a difficult decision. One stormy night in December, the padre returned from the hut of one of the mission families, where the father lay very ill with a high fever, and had been prepared for death. In a few minutes the man's son, who had been confirmed recently, came running breathlessly to the mission office.

"Padre," he panted, as the drops of rain ran down his dusky face, "my father says he cannot die without being confirmed. He says he would be ashamed before God to know that his son had received the Sacrament, and he had not. He has been attending the classes, too. Padre, will you give it to him before he goes to God?"

Junípero stared at the boy's pleading face, while the struggle went on in his mind. Which was more important, the arrogant order of a military governor, or the Grace of God given to a man about to stand before his Maker?

190

A minute or two later, carefully carrying the holy oil beneath his robe, the Father President hurried along with the boy to the hut. With them was Juan Crespi to act as sponsor for the dying man.

"Perhaps I have done wrong, Fray," Junípero said later as he and Fray Juan crossed the courtyard to their own door. "I have disobeyed the command of the civil authority, but I am sure it was right to do it, for I know that my permit is valid."

Fray Juan nodded. "In the eyes of God you have done what is right," he said firmly.

Later, there were other cases where Padre Serra brought the Sacrament to someone on the point of death, firm in his belief that the wishes of God take precedence over all earthly rulings.

Almost a whole year had passed before a letter came from de Croix saying that he had been told by the Viceroy that Padre Serra was not to be prevented from confirming, and that he was to have a soldier guard whenever he wished to go from one mission to another.

With a prayer of thanks ever on his lips, Junípero began confirming again in his own mission in September of the year 1781. After a trip to San Antonio, he announced that he would leave soon for Santa Clara and San Francisco.

"I have a wish to go with you." Fray Juan Crespi told him. "I have not seen the port of our father, Saint Francis, since I saw it with the exploring party in 1769, soon after we came to California. Then, too, I feel that I should like to see my old school friend, Fray Francisco Palou, again. I am now sixty-two. You are older than that, I know, but the years weigh more heavily on my shoulders. Who knows? I may not have another chance to be with our good brother from Majorca."

The kindly October sun shone down in warmth on the

two old padres in their worn gray robes and sandaled feet as they trod the trail through the smiling plain of the River Guadalupe. Their shoulders were bent now, and their steps were slow, but nothing could dim the boldness of spirit with which they trudged on over the weary miles.

They stopped at Santa Clara, and promised to help lay the cornerstone for the new church on their return. Fray Juan marveled at the well-laid-out fields and clustered huts of San Jose. With lagging steps, but high spirits and bright eyes, they came, after two days, to the shining sand dunes with their clumps of sweet-smelling mint and rosemary that stretched about the walls of the mission on Laguna Dolores. Fray Francisco met them far down the road, with smiling face, and an arm thrown about each of their shoulders.

What happiness the three friars found in the fortnight that they were together! Each night, long after the sharp fog had drifted in from the sea, or the pale moon shone down on the lonely mission huts, they sat talking. Once again they lived over the days in Majorca when, as teacher and students, they had come to know each other. They recounted their journeys to the New World, and the missionary years in Mexico. They dwelt for a long time on the days when they three had been so happily together at Carmel after Junípero's return from Mexico. When the talks were finished, each in his own way gave thanks for the bright ribbon of friendship that had been allowed to twine itself through their hard missionary lives.

When the Sacrament had been given to all the converts prepared to receive it, Junípero and Juan took their leave. Unshed tears shone in all their eyes as Francisco said, "The pain of parting is as great as the joy of your arrival."

For two of them, it was the final parting in this world. A few days after returning to Carmel, Fray Juan became very ill, and knew that he was being called by his Maker. Happy in the knowledge that the hand which gave him the Last Sacrament was that of Junípero, he closed his eyes forever on New Year's Day, 1782. Junípero had his friend's body placed in the church on the Gospel side of the altar, so that he might remain always in the place he had loved. The padre never ceased to miss his faithful companion's help and presence.

The church built in 1811 at Mission San Buenaventura, founded March 31, 1782.

San Buenaventura—at Last!

"The procession of missions," Padre Serra used to say,
"is very disconnected; to be agreeable to God and man
it must march in succession, and the gaps must be filled."

For most of the thirteen years he had been in California, Junípero had been awaiting the word which came to
him in February of 1782. San Buenaventura was to be
founded, at last! One of the gaps in the procession would
be filled. This was the mission that the Inspector-General,
Don José de Gálvez, had said was to be "his" mission,
before the expedition set out for California. The padre
could see the great man now, packing the bells and candle
sticks, the altar cloths and vestments to be used in "his"
mission church. It was to have been one of the first to be
started, but the years had gone on, and its founding had
been delayed by the military commanders under one pre-
text or another. Gálvez himself had gone back to Spain,

where he held the high office of Minister General of the Indies. Now, at long last, "his" mission was to come into being.

As soon as he received the letter from Governor Neve, the Father President left for the south. He stopped at San Luis Obispo and San Antonio to give Confirmation. As he passed through the Santa Bárbara region, where the new mission was to be built, he gave many presents to the people, telling them that he would soon return with other padres who would live among them.

One night, long after the soft, star-pricked darkness had wrapped the land, he came to the silver trickle of the River Porciuncula, where a pueblo had been started a few months before.

"*Porciuncula!*" he said to the soldiers of his guard. "It is a small portion of water, indeed. Fray Juan was right. It was our beloved Juan Crespi who named this stream, you know."

"When was that, Padre?" one of the soldiers asked.

"Shortly after we had arrived in California. Juan Crespi went with Portolá on the expedition from San Diego to look for the Bay of Monterey. They passed along this way, and when Fray saw the small amount of water in this river, he was reminded of an incident in the life of Saint Francis."

"What was the incident?" he was asked.

"Not long after Francis Bernardone started his life of poverty and good works, other men from Assisi began to join him, and they formed a sort of brotherhood. Since they owned nothing at all, they had no place to hold divine services when the weather was bad. A friend of Francis's, a Benedictine abbot, offered him a tiny chapel belonging to the Benedictine Order. Our spiritual father did not think he could remain true to the vow of poverty he had taken if he accepted it. The Abbot pointed out to him, though, that his order believed in sharing with others. Therefore, Francis would not be owning, but merely sharing, the chapel of the Benedictines. On this understanding, the founder of our Franciscan Order was willing to use the chapel. He and his 'Little Poor Men of Assisi' named it 'Our Lady of Porciuncula' because it was so small. It always remained the place they liked best to go. Now this pueblo so far away from Assisi in Italy is being called by the same name, 'Nuestra Señora, Reina de los Angeles de Porciuncula' (Our Lady, Queen of the Angels on the Porciuncula).

"It is already being called just 'Los Angeles,' I hear," put in one of the soldiers, "because the name is so long."

"Yes. 'Los Angeles' it will be, I am sure," the padre told him.

Some distance beyond the little river a ditch had been dug, bringing water from upstream. Between the two streams lay the settlers' newly plowed fields. The road led directly into the plaza of the little town. No alcalde greeted the padre and his guard here, as had been the case at San Jose. However, the people all came out of their huts, which were built around the plaza, and welcomed their guests.

"This is our town hall, Your Reverence, where you may stay for the night. Just beside it is the barracks, where your guard may find shelter," one of the Spaniards of the town told him.

Junípero was surprised to find that of the forty-four settlers who had come from Mexico to begin this pueblo, only two were Spaniards. The others were Negroes of full blood or half-castes, or Mexican Indians. The Father President said Mass for them in the morning, and then left for San Gabriel, about twelve miles away.

He found Governor Neve waiting at San Gabriel with all the soldiers who had been sent from Mexico for the three missions to be founded in the Santa Bárbara region. A week later the large expedition set forth. As the order to start echoed along the line of march, Junípero was reminded of the caravan under Portolá, with which he had first come to California.

"¡Vamonos!" shouted an officer of the guards, and the long line slowly began to move. At the head rode Governor Neve with his personal guard of ten soldiers from Monterey. The seventy soldiers and officers who were to be assigned to the new missions came next, with their families and a few San Gabriel converts. Junípero and Padre Cambón were the only priests, and they followed. The servants and mule boys with the pack animals brought up the rear, as the long line started for the coast to the north.

"Well," Junípero remarked to Fray Cambón, "it has taken thirteen years to found this mission, but it is being done with much splendor, at last."

At midnight the first night, when all were sleeping in their tents, pounding hoofbeats along the trail broke the quiet, as a messenger came riding in haste from San Gabriel. Don Pedro Fages had arrived to talk with the Governor about the Indian raids on two missions on the Colorado River, where missionaries and settlers had been killed. Neve, with his personal guard, left at once for San Gabriel. The rest of the expedition went on and three days later came to the place which had been chosen long ago for the Mission of San Buenaventura.

The sunlight sparkled on a little cove where many large Indian canoes were moored. Nearby was a good-sized village of cone-shaped grass huts that looked like haystacks. Beyond the wide beach bordering the cove, the party came to a halt, and made camp.

On Easter Sunday, March 31, 1782, Junípero blessed the ground and the cross which had been set up. He then

The Carmel Mission as Captain George Vancouver saw it in 1794.

said Mass, with Padre Cambón acting as the choir, and took possession of the mission, while the black, beady eyes of the village Indians watched everything that went on. The padres gave trinkets to the pagans, who were willing to help in building the chapel and padres' house. The soldiers started constructing their barracks and houses, as well as a stockade around the whole mission for protection. A ditch, too, was begun, to bring water from a stream not far away.

In two weeks Governor Neve rejoined the expedition. Leaving a guard of fifteen soldiers with Padre Cambón at the new mission, Junípero, the Governor, and the rest of the soldiers went on to Santa Bárbara.

The warm touch of the sunlight and the sweet scent of the light spring breezes traveled with them as they traced the coast line to the north. Just off shore in the mists on the left were the Channel Islands, so called because between them and the mainland a channel was formed. When they had gone about twenty-seven miles, they came to another large Indian village. Here the Governor called a halt, while he, with the Father President and some of the soldiers, explored the region.

About a mile from the beach which bordered the bay, they found a high grassy spot looking out over the water. Here, with the close-by mountains as a background, the soldiers began to cut trees for the cross, the altar table, and hut to be used as a chapel. On April 21, 1782, the first Mass was said, and possession was taken for the Santa Bárbara Presidio.

Day after day Junípero expected the Governor to give the order to start the mission, but Neve said nothing. Finally, the padre asked, "Do you not think, Your Honor, that the Mission of Santa Bárbara can be started now?"

"No, Padre. I have decided not to begin the mission until the presidio is finished."

Junípero was disappointed, of course. The presidio should be finished soon, though, he thought, and he would stay there until it was, so that he could witness the filling of one more gap in the mission procession.

During his stay, there was a serious confrontation with Neve, but the padre never revealed exactly what happened. In a letter to the Father Guardian of the College of San Fernando, he wrote, "He began by stripping me of my powers. After that—but I neither can nor wish to recount to you what I saw and heard during those three weeks." Later, he wrote to a fellow Franciscan, "When I tried, as was my duty, to inform the College, the pen fell from my hand."

When it was apparent that the work on the presidio would not go forward, and that the mission would not be built, he decided to go back to Carmel. There he would await the arrival of the ships with the six missionaries who were to be sent from San Fernando. When they arrived, he would send a priest down here to Santa Bárbara. In the meantime, one of the missionaries from San Juan Capistrano would come.

More slowly than ever before, the old padre put the weary miles to the north behind him. Confirmation was given at San Luis Obispo and San Antonio. Then he trod that well-loved stretch of the California trail that would bring him to his own Carmel. As he neared Monterey, a messenger on horseback rode to meet him.

"The ships have come, Your Reverence," he told the padre as he alighted from his horse.

The tired old eyes gleamed with pleasure. "And the six missionaries have arrived from San Fernando, have they?" he asked eagerly.

"No, Padre, no missionaries came, at all."

Junípero's shoulders drooped, and he was suddenly very weary as he began to read the letters the messenger had just handed him.

The letter from the Father Guardian of San Fernando explained why the missionaries had not come. They had been about ready to leave when they heard that all the new missions to be started in California were to follow a new plan, drawn up by de Croix and Neve. According to this plan, the missionaries were to have no gifts of clothing and trinkets to offer the Indians. The missions would not grow crops, or have shops, and the Indians were to live in their own villages. The missionaries and the college authorities knew that it would be impossible to win the pagans to Christianity without gifts to offer, or to attempt to civilize them if they were not to live at the missions. Therefore, the friars had asked to be excused from coming to California. The Father Guardian told Padre Serra not to found any new residence missions until the Commandant General de Croix changed the plan, and allowed

Interior of restored cell at the Carmel Mission where Father Serra lived and died.

them to operate under the old system, which had been so successful.

As he limped along the road toward Carmel, Junípero reflected that at the two missions on the Colorado River where the raids had taken place, the Indians were living in their villages, supporting themselves as they had before their conversion. It was, no doubt, due to the fact that the missionary fathers had charge only of spiritual work there, and thus had no control over the Indians, that the dreadful massacres had happened. How glad he was that no California missions had been started on those terms.

Then, like a knife thrust, came a distressing thought. San Buenaventura was one of the new missions. Neve had said nothing about the new system when he arrived from San Gabriel to find the fields set out, and workshops and converts' houses planned. Still, he, Junípero, had expected to have two missionaries from the College of San Fernando to send there. Not only were they not coming, but he had orders from the Father Guardian not to found any more missions. Should he suspend San Buenaventura, after all these years of waiting to see it come into being? If he did, would he not be preventing many, many souls from becoming Christians? If he did not, would he be disobeying the Father Guardian's order?

The question haunted him night and day after his return to Carmel. He resolved to have the ideas of his brother Franciscans on the matter. So, from Mission Dolores and Santa Clara, from San Antonio and San Luis Obispo, the padres came at the Father President's call. When they had all discussed the problem fully, they decided that San Buenaventura should remain because it had been founded before the Father Guardian's order came, and would be conducted under the old system. Moreover, there were two missionaries who could be sent there, although that would leave Junípero alone at Carmel.

He watched the padres leave for their own posts with a sense of relief that the matter was settled, and a prayer of thanks that the decision had been what he had hoped it would be. Having to give up a mission already started would have been almost more than he could have borne.

Since there was no other priest at San Carlos, the Father President could not leave until the two missionaries he had asked for should come from Mexico. For the present he could make no more trips to visit the other missions to give Confirmation.

The days were not long enough to do all that was to be done at Carmel, though. More and more Indians were asking to be taken into the mission. At one time a whole village arrived, its headman leading the way. Not long after, all the people of another village came, asking to be baptized. These pagans had to learn the prayers, and to have lessons in the Catechism before they could be taken into the Church. How Junípero missed Fray Juan, who had once taken over so many of the mission tasks!

In addition to overseeing all the other activities of the mission, Padre Serra was having large blocks of stone cut from a quarry in the hills. It was brought to Carmel by the Indians, and stored for the day when a new church should be started. The old one was no longer large enough for all the converts, and it was the dream of the Father President to construct a fine stone church, large and beautiful.

In the autumn another government change saw Pedro Fages, the former enemy of the missionaries, back in Monterey as governor, replacing Neve. With Fages came his wife and son, Pedrito.

As the months wore on, and spring followed winter, Junípero felt that he had not much more time on this earth to finish his work for Christ. For many years he had had a pain in his chest, but now it was very severe, and brought with it spells of choking and suffocation. His old-time strength seemed to fail him since his last journey from the south.

The arrival of the supply ship in June, bringing the two missionaries he had requested, gave new energy to the feeble padre. A last flicker of the old ardent gleam flared in the fading dark eyes. Now that he could leave one of the new priests at Carmel, he must be off on a tour of the missions. His permit to give Confirmation would expire in July of the following year. He must confirm as many as possible by that time. When the ship sailed for San Diego in August, Junípero stood on deck watching the rugged headlands of the bay fade into the distance.

For the last time the dust of the California trails held the imprint of Junípero's sandaled feet. Never again, he knew, would he tread that road under the open sky, beside the pounding sea, through the fair valleys and over the rounding hills. Much of the trail, with its nine mission stations, he had made himself. It became, on this last journey, a pathway of memories of the past, and a track of hope for the future.

A hot sun shone down on the brown hills and yellow beaches of San Diego, as it had fourteen years ago, when he had looked on that harbor for the first time. He remembered how his imagination had soared then as he realized that this was the gateway to the great adventure of winning California to God and civilization. Well, the adventure had been rewarding, surely, though not so completely as he had wished. The gateway itself had, from the very beginning, been destined to trouble. It had seen death from disease and murder. It had known fire and looting, cruelty and excommunication, and for a long time, the hostility and stubbornness of the Indians. Now, however, the pagan hearts had been softened, and many natives had finally come to the mission. Junípero gave a special prayer of thanks that there were more than two hundred ready to be confirmed. He thought of the first long months spent at San Diego when not a single one had appeared to be baptized.

It was September when he had reached the southern mission on this last journey. On the 14th of that month he celebrated an anniversary. Fifty-three years before, in the city of Palma, he had taken the Franciscan habit for the first time. The robe and cowl had brought him the suffering and hardship he had eagerly accepted when he had put them on. They had also brought the unbounded delights of a life of service to the Creator and His children. Try as he might, the aged priest could not imagine having lived any other kind of life, for no other would have had any meaning in the end.

Before leaving San Diego, he went to the first mission site on the hill overlooking the lazy waters of the bay. There was the palm tree he had placed in the earth himself, now grown to a good size. Near it was the first grape vine to be planted in California. Oh, San Diego was dear to him, indeed. Like an unruly child, it had caused him many heartaches, it was true, but it was the first of his missions, and no other would ever be quite like it.

"Father President," Padre Lasuén said to him as he was about to start on his journey northward, "I beg of you to stay a few days longer with us, and rest. The trouble in your chest is much too severe for you to begin that long trip now."

"Many, many thanks, Fray Fermín, for your kindness, but I must go now. I cannot know how much longer I have to live, and I must give the Sacrament of Confirmation to all the Christians in all the missions before the permit expires, or I am called out of this world."

"Then, at least, you can take one of our sure-footed mules to carry you to San Juan Capistrano. I fear that you will not be able to make the trip, otherwise."

"No, Padre, many thanks again, but I have resolved to make this last journey as I have all the others—on foot," he feeble old man replied. "God will give me strength."

So, on a blue October day, he left the spot where he had first raised the cross in California. Though the pain in his chest made every drawn breath an agony, he could not help enjoying the loveliness of that strip of southern coastline where the throbbing Pacific traces her outline with a finger dipped in beauty. Two days after leaving San Diego, the little party made up of the padre and his soldier guards rounded Point Juan, and turned from the ocean into the inviting valley that held the sunny mission of San Juan Capistrano.

After pausing to kneel before the cross, Junípero pointed to a little mound nearby. "There is the spot," he said, "where the bells were found after being buried for more than a year when San Diego was attacked."

The tiny church had been enlarged five years before to hold its every-growing number of converts. Now, its congregation was outgrowing it again, as could be seen when more than two hundred were confirmed before Junípero left.

"One day we hope to have a fine stone church at San Juan," the missionaries told the Father President.

They pointed out to him with pride, too, their flocks of sheep and goats dotting the green pasture lands beyond the buildings. The vineyard, where vines from Mexico had been grafted on the wild ones which grew all about, became larger each year.

He left San Juan one morning at daybreak on his way to San Gabriel.

Many weary travelers who had come to California over Anza's Trail had blessed the first sight of Mission San Gabriel, but none more heartily than did Fray Junípero on his way from San Juan Capistrano. His choking spells had been so bad that both he and the soldiers of his guard had feared that each breath might be the last. When, at length, the gates came into view, the exhausted padre offered a tiny prayer of thanks, and staggered into the mission haven. Once there, however, he insisted on confirming the converts at once, and saying Mass, as usual.

One morning after Mass, a small Indian boy who had served at the altar, came to Padre Cruzado of that mission. His eyes were full of tears. "Padre," he said, "surely the 'old padre' wants to die."

Instead, though, the "old padre" had great joy in confirming so many converts in this mission, whose people had been distrustful of the Spaniards in the early days because of the actions of the soldiers. In all, eight hundred sixty-six had been given the Sacrament here since the beginning. Our Lady of Sorrows, whose picture had calmed the rioting savages on the day the mission site was chosen, had been responsible for the progress at San Gabriel, Junípero believed.

Not only in religious ways had this mission prospered, however. All about in this autumn of 1873 were grain fields yellow with stubble. The grain itself was being threshed in a cleared space where the earth was hard and smooth. The Indian men were driving horses around and around over the wheat to break it into small pieces.

Then the women would put some stalks in their bright-colored baskets. When they tossed the baskets in the air, the light stalks blew away, leaving the heavier heads of grain to fall to the ground. San Gabriel raised more grain than any other mission. On its wide pasture lands thousands of cattle and horses grazed. The missionary fathers had planted a fine orchard, too, and many olive trees.

"San Gabriel is the garden spot of our mission chain," the Father President told its missionaries. "I leave you content in knowing that from your ample harvests, you can, if need be, help the other missions which are not so favored."

Junípero was eager to go on to San Buenaventura, his youngest station, founded only the year before. Though the choking and pain in his chest were very bad, he set out as soon as all had been confirmed at San Gabriel. The journey of ninety long miles was almost more than the sick, lame, old man could stand. Each night, as he lay down to rest beneath the stars, his soldier guard feared that he would not be able to rise the next morning. Each day he called up all his courage, though, and finally the sight of the sturdy Indian canoes riding the waves told the travelers that San Buenaventura was not far off. When the sound of hammering and cutting came down the trail, Junípero even hastened his weary steps. Soon the partly-built church was before him, and he hurried to raise his hand in blessing over some Indians carrying timbers on their shoulders for the building.

"What progress you have made here since last year!" he told the priests happily, as they showed him the stone irrigation ditch the Indians had begun to make, and the fields cleared and planted with fruit trees, as well as vegetables, and all enclosed by an adobe wall.

The Father President's greatest pleasure came when

he was told that twenty-two natives had been baptized. "Thanks be to God," he cried, "that in this region where, a year ago, there were only pagans, there is now the beginning of a Christian settlement."

He seemed to feel better at once, and after leaving the mission, he visited about twenty Indian villages in the vicinity of Santa Bárbara. With a crowd of children always at his side, he went from one town to the next, giving small gifts to the people, and making signs of friendship. It was plain to see that these were the most intelligent and advanced among the California tribes. Junípero was so saddened to think that he had not been allowed to start a mission among them to teach the ways of civilization and of God, that the tears were often falling from his eyes. His prayer as he left the area was, "O Lord, send workers into this vineyard that they may gather the harvest for Thee."

The winter rains had begun long before San Luis Obispo was reached. The old padre was thankful that he had felt better since leaving San Buenaventura, for he and his guards were often wet to the skin, while the chill winds from the mountains whirled about them. One of these mountains which almost encircled the Valley of the Bears always made Junípero think of a bishop's hat—perhaps the hat of Saint Louis, Bishop of Toulouse himself, for whom the mission was named.

The friars came to the gateway to meet Padre Serra. As he walked with them to their house, he noticed smoke rising from an outdoor oven beyond the kitchen. A mission Indian was putting something into the oven with a long handled paddle.

"What is he baking?" asked the Father President, always interested in anything being done in his missions.

Tiles," answered the San Luis priest. "At least, we hope they will be proper tiles one day. So far, we have not been able to bake them without cracking, but we are trying a different way of mixing the clay now. Perhaps these will be better.''

"You expect to use them for roofs for the mission buildings, do you?'' Junípero asked.

"Yes, Padre. You remember that we have had three fires here, set by unfriendly Indians who shot burning arrows into our tule and grass roofs. We decided that we must have fireproof ones, such as the tile roofs of Mexico and our own Spain. Nobody knows exactly how to make them, though. We have been experimenting. Come, let me show you.''

Junípero watched curiously as an Indian placed sand over a stripped log, and colored it with a red clay mixture. This he smoothed and molded over the log.

"We shall have to wait for a sunny day to dry it,'' the missionary said. "After it is dry, we put it in the oven, and bake it.''

"This is very interesting,'' Junípero told him. "When you have perfected the making of them, we must have red tiles on all the buildings of all the missions.''

On leaving, he looked at the record book of Baptisms and Confirmations. Although San Luis was not a large mission, the book showed that six hundred sixteen Indians had become Christians since the days when Don Padre Fages had led his bear hunt in this valley. "Well done,'' the Father President said to the missionaries as he bade them farewell, and left for San Antonio.

Mud from the recent rains was knee-deep on the trail they made in and out among mountains whose peaks were often frosted with white. Padre Serra and his little group of soldiers plodded along, often sliding and falling in the mire. Finally, after coming through a slippery, dangerous pass, they dropped down into the green, pleasant valley where San Antonio de Padua nestled. It was dusk, and as they neared the mission, the sweet tones of the Angelus rang through the crisp air, and echoed among the clumps of oaks.

Junípero hurried through the gates to the church, and up the adobe steps of the bell tower. "Let me ring them just once," he begged of the astonished Indian who clung to the dangling rope.

A look of childish happiness was on the old padre's face as, in spite of his weariness from the day's journey, he tugged at the heavy rope. He was living again the time twelve years before, when he had first come to this lovely spot, and had been suddenly filled with a desire to call all the pagans in the vicinity to come and hear the word of God.

Then, only one wary *Gentile* had peered from behind a tree at the bell's sound. Now, the courtyard teemed with converts leaving their day's work at the call of the Angelus. At this time, San Antonio had over one thousand Christian Indians living within its walls—more than any other mission.

"It is well that the soil of San Antonio produces such good crops," Padre Serra said to one of the missionaries, "when the Lord has blessed it with so many converts."

"One reason it yields so much is because of Padre Sitjar's irrigation system," was the reply. He pointed out the miles of ditches bringing water to the orchards and fields from a reservoir which, in turn, was fed by stone ditches from the San Antonio River. "With plenty of water we can grow almost anything. Have you ever seen the pears from our orchard? They are the largest I have ever seen."

"Yes, the fame of your pears has reached my ears," smiled the Father President, "though I have never seen them."

"Over there," the Franciscan went on, "Padre Sitjar

212

Etching by H. Chapman Ford

Irrigation was developed at most missions by the Padres. This aqueduct was at Santa Barbara Mission but has been torn down.

has started to build a mill to grind our wheat into flour."

"It will be the first one in California!" Padre Serra exclaimed.

Before leaving, he inspected the tannery, where the mission Indians tanned the hides from their own animals. He stole a few hours, too, to browse through the large library the padres were collecting.

Then, when San Antonio's two hundred converts had

been confirmed, Junípero left for his own mission. A group of children walked with him for a distance down the road, as they had at every station. When it was time for them to go back, they left their beloved old padre with many backward glances and smiles. On their lips was the tender phrase he had taught them: "Amar á Dios, old padre, amar á Dios." How it echoed back to him along five hundred miles of California trails: "Amar á Dios"—as its meaning had rung out along the whole road of his life—"Love God."

XXIII
The Trail Ends

Once, long before, Junípero had lingered in his native village of Petra to share the joys of Easter with the people of his old home before leaving on his journey to the New World. Now, it brought him happiness to pass the holy season again with his own people in Carmel, the only other spot that he had ever called home, before he should set out on another journey to an unknown world, as he knew he must.

But there was still work for him to do. Only a few months remained before his Confirmation permit would expire. The two northern missions had yet to be visited. The month of May was just beginning as he journeyed through the open plains around Santa Clara. The tender green of grass and trees sparkled in the sunlight, while gay yellow patches of wild mustard laughed up from the meadows, and here and there delicate blue, pink, or white blossoms peered from the shade of an overhanging rock. In spite of his seventy years, Junípero felt young and happy as he looked at them, though his steps lagged pitifully along the way.

Leaving Santa Clara to be visited on his return, when he was to dedicate the new church, he went straight on to San Francisco, where Fray Francisco met him with open arms. "You must come in and rest after your tiring journey," Fray Francisco said.

"Not until I have seen the work that has been done on the new church," was Junípero's reply.

"I laid the first stone two years ago, on April 25th," Francisco told him as they looked at the adobe building slowly taking shape, "and since then, our Indians have worked very hard on it. Many years will pass before it is finished, though. We have also started a vegetable garden. You cannot see it from here. We had to go some distance to find good soil and a protected spot. Our orchard here is doing well, though. Soon it will give us figs, apricots, peaches, and pomegranates."

As the friars went into the mission office, Junípero noticed that Francisco's rough pine desk was strewn with papers.

"It is not very tidy, I'm afraid," Francisco said. "I am setting down all the notes I have taken on the happenings since the first expedition came to California. You remember I had started to do this at Carmel."

"Is it to be a book?" Junípero asked.

"Perhaps," his friend replied. "It seemed to me that our brothers at the College of San Fernando might be interested in reading of what happened here."

"It will be a valuable work, Fray—a true history of the colonization of California. It may be that people who live here in generations to come will be glad to read it, too."

"At any rate, it will be a record for anyone to read who

is interested,'' Francisco Palou finished.

Each time he had come to this spot where his old friend labored, Junípero had felt refreshed. Its cool, bright days and crisp, foggy nights seemed to cleanse his soul. The sharp, clean smell from the nearby fields of mint lifted his spirit. On this trip, the brisk, fresh breezes from the ocean tended to sweep away all the cares and troubles of his life, leaving his mind free for the things of the life to come. His worries over the lack of missionaries, the governor's actions, the new mission plan, all seemed to drop away from him here, so that he could accept the Lord's offer: "Come to me, all ye that are heavy-burdened, and I will refresh you.''

With this sense of being free from the earthly chains that had bound him, Padre Serra performed the rite of Confirmation for all the converts and then went on to Santa Clara, where Fray Francisco had gone a few days before.

Santa Clara's new adobe church was the finest at any mission. Its great beams had been brought on the shoulders of the Indians from the redwood forests of the Santa Cruz Mountains. Its ceiling was painted with a mixture of red rock and cactus juice. The natives had used their own designs which showed streaks of lightning, bright flowers, birds, and the wavy lines of the "River of Life.''

"You have the most beautiful church in California,'' the Father President told the mission Indians, "and your bright paintings are a joy to behold. How happy you must be to know that you have made God's house a place of beauty!''

All the Christian Indians, with many more who were still pagans, were present when Junípero blessed the church, and dedicated it to Santa Clara, the young woman of Assisi who followed in the footsteps of Saint Francis.

The Governor was there, also, as well as the troops and settlers of the pueblo of San Jose.

The Father President gave Confirmation in the new church the day after its dedication. When the ceremony was over, one of the converts, a young girl, came into the sacristy. "Old Padre," she said, "my mother was baptized a few months ago, but she still lives in the village. She is very sick, and could not come to the church today. She does not want to die without receiving the Sacrament. Could you come to the village, and confirm her? There is a baptized child there, too, who is ill. His parents want him confirmed, also."

Making the sign of the cross on the girl's forehead, Junípero said, "If you will show me the way to your village, we shall go at once. No one is to be left without this Sacrament."

So, to be sure that all who were prepared received it, he went to the village homes of any who could not come to the church.

He asked Fray Francisco to stay with him for a few days at Santa Clara, and then he left for his own mission. Slowly and painfully the tired old man made his way to Monterey. Looking out over the gray-green bay, he let his glance touch all the well-remembered spots of his first days there. Here was the point where his small boat had run up on the sand, and where he had first stepped on these beloved shores of the Bay of Monterey. To the left, beautiful in its springtime green, was Vizcaíno's oak, its branches spreading to the place where he had first offered up the holy sacrifice of the Mass. There on the headland still stood the great cross put there by Portolá's first exploring party, and which Junípero had seen from the ship as it entered the bay. As he watched, the golden sun, close to setting, sprang into crimson tinted glory from behind a cloud, brushing each loved spot with a fringe of light. It was as if the glow from thousands of heavenly candles touched all the enduring landmarks to impress them on the mind and heart of him who might never see them again. Junípero bowed his head. "Oh Lord, I am not worthy," he said, "to witness such beauty on this earth."

With this glory in his soul, and the breath of salt air in his nostrils, he limped over the pine-scented hills and through the sweet valleys of that often-traveled five miles to Carmel. Far from his own gate the first of his people came to meet him. With loving hands his Indians led him back to San Carlos. As he stumbled into the familiar courtyard, his sigh was a prayer of thanks that he had been allowed the precious boon of returning to his own dear Carmel to die.

There were a few still to be confirmed. When the permit expired on July 16th, he sat down at his desk and added the neatly written sums in the large book before him. Five thousand, three hundred, seven was the total of persons to whom he had given the Sacrament of Confirmation, and some five hundred more had been baptized at all the missions in California. Thoughtfully, he lifted the heavy leather cover of the book, and closed it. It was as if he were closing the book of his life. He shook his head slowly, thinking of the untold numbers of the *Gentiles* he had not been able to bring to God. Then, with an expression that seemed resigned to accepting things as they were, and with outspread hands, he appeared to be offering the volume to the Heavenly Father.

The end of the month brought news that once would have been most welcome. Neve had granted permission for the founding of Santa Bárbara! Now, it scarcely touched him, for he knew that he would never see the new mission, whose building he had hoped for so desperately. Santa Bárbara would be the concern of those who came after him.

Junípero had no other priest with him now at San Carlos, and the old ghost of loneliness came to haunt him again. Now was the time, he thought, when he needed company. When life was nearing its close, every human being wanted the nearness of someone who had been dear to him.

A letter to Francisco Palou in San Francisco, was followed, as soon as possible, by the good man's appearance at Carmel. He found his old friend suffering greatly from the feeling of suffocation and heaviness in his chest. On the evening of his arrival, Junípero went to the church for Vespers, as usual. In the closing hymn to the Blessed Mother, his voice rang out firm and natural.

"The Father President does not seem very sick," Francisco said to a soldier standing near him.

"We must not be too hopeful," the soldier replied. "He is sick, but when it comes to praying and singing, he always seems well. Really, it is almost over for him."

That night, when it was time for Junípero to go to rest, there was no blanket on the two boards he used as a bed. Having seen it earlier, Fray Francisco asked, "Where is your blanket, Fray?"

Junípero looked a bit shame-faced. "I gave it away," he admitted.

Francisco could guess where it had gone, for he had recognized one of the visitors that day, and had remembered something that had taken place years before. One of the supply ships coming to Monterey had brought as passengers a mother hen and her brood of chicks. The captain had given them to Padre Serra, who had hoped to start a flock with them. They were the only chickens in California, and he was proud to have them. One dark night they disappeared from their coop. The theft was traced to an Indian woman and her small son. When accused, the woman had said that she and her boy were hungry, that she was sorry, and would never steal again. Of course, the padre had forgiven her, but he had never quite forgotten the happening. That day, the mother, now an old woman, had visited the sick priest.

Francisco smiled fondly at his old friend, "Were you paying her for the chickens?" he asked.

"I felt that I wanted to give her something, and the blanket was the only thing I had," he said, as a blush came to his sunken cheeks. "Now the whole thing is forgotten."

The next day he asked Francisco to say Mass, as he did not feel well enough, but he sang in the choir as he had in those far-off childhood years on Majorca. Some bolts of blue cloth had just come on the ship, and he spent much of the day cutting out garments for his beloved charges.

Finally, a day came when he felt so weak that he told Fray Francisco he wished to receive Holy Viaticum—the last Communion. "I shall go to the church to receive it," he announced in a muffled voice.

"But you cannot do that. You are not able, and besides, it is never done. We can adorn your room, and make it presentable for the coming of our Lord here," Francisco told him.

The words of the psalm which he had said thousands of times in the Mass and which always found a response in his soul, came to him: "I have loved, O Lord, the beauty of Thy house, and the place where Thy glory dwelleth." Yes, he had loved the beauty of the Lord's house, whether it was the convent church of Petra, the great cathedrals of Palma and Mexico City, or the crude altar within a brushwood shelter on the shores of California. But most of all, perhaps, he had loved this house of the Lord he had helped to build with his own hands, here in this

spot so dear to his heart. In it he would receive his Lord for the last time. "I will go to the church," he said firmly.

There, with his people and the soldiers from the presidio about him, he took Communion. Then, though the tears streamed down his face, he sang in a natural voice the Benediction hymn, "Tantum Ergo."

When, the next day, he heard that some old friends of his, officers of the ship anchored in the bay, were coming along the road to San Carlos, he had the bells rung. He welcomed the men standing upright at his door, as he always had done when visitors came to see him. With his usual courtesy, he told them how glad he was to see them, and listened to the stories of their recent voyages to Peru. As they were leaving, he said, "It gives me great happiness that you have come so great a distance to throw a little earth on my grave."

Shortly after noon the next day, when the sick priest had read the Divine Office, Fray Francisco asked him to

222

Interior of Mission Carmel where Father Junipero Serra was buried in front of the altar. He lies in the center with Father Crespi to the left and Father Lausen to the right. Father Lopez lies to the far left but not in the picture.

take a little broth. When it was finished, Padre Serra said, "Let us now go to rest."

So saying, he lay on his bed of boards with the crucifix resting above his heart. Years before, he had set out on a long journey with the cross of Christ as his only possession. He had now set out on the longest journey of all with the same cross clasped in his arms. When Fray Francisco came into the room some time later, he knew that his dear old friend would never again come to port on earthly shores. With a smile of peace on his face, he had gone to rest in the Lord on that afternoon of August 29th, 1784, at the age of seventy.

As soon as the tolling of the mission bell told the Indians that their dear father had left them, they began coming in a never-ending line with bunches of blue, yellow, and pink wild flowers from the woods. Touching his hands and face, they would murmur, "Holy father! Blessed father!" while their tears flowed. Everyone who knew him wanted something that had belonged to him. Francisco Palou had to station guards around the coffin to prevent people from cutting a piece of his robe, a bit of a handkerchief, or a lock of hair.

On the day of burial, the cannon on the ship boomed every half hour, answered by one from the presidio. The mission bells, which he had rung so often on occasions of joy, tolled throughout the day. Since all the officers, soldiers, and sailors wanted to be allowed to help carry the coffin, the procession went slowly around the wide courtyard twice, stopping every few feet to change bearers. Finally, amid the sobs and tears of his "children," he was laid to rest on the Gospel side of the altar beside Juan Crespi, as he had asked to be.

Thus, within a crude mission on the edge of the wilderness, to the sound of the wailing of his simple "brown brothers," one of the great men of our country was laid to rest. He might have become one of the finest scholars of his age, known and respected all over Europe. Almost surely he could have held a high place in the Church, where he would have been honored and revered. Had he elected such a life, the great and famous people of his time would have honored him at his death with costly flowers and fine speeches. Instead, he had chosen to give his life to the uncivilized natives of a land distant from his own, where he knew that heavy toil, hardships, and suffering would be his lot.

Now that his life was over, the recognition he received was the sincere sorrow and undying love and gratitude of a simple, childlike people whom he had taught to be Christians. That was what he would have treasured most, for he always lived up to the motto of the Order of Saint Francis: "God forbid that I should glory, save in the cross of our Lord, Jesus Christ."

Bibliography

Ainsworth, Katherine. *In the Shade of the Juniper Tree.* Doubleday & Co., 1970.

Bancroft, Hubert Howe. *History of California.* San Francisco, 1886.

History of Mexico. San Francisco, 1883.

Bandini, Albert R. *Fray Junipero of California.* Carmel, 1949.

Beilharz, Edwin A. *Felipe de Neve, First Governor of California.* California Historical Society, 1971.

Bolton, Herbert F. *Fray Juan Crespi, Missionary Explorer.*

Bolton, Hubert F. *Spanish Exploration in the Southwest.* New York, 1916.

Caughey, John Walton. *California.* New York, 1940.

Chapman, Charles E. *The Founding of Spanish California.* New York, 1916.

History of California: The Spanish Period. New York, 1921.

Clinch, Bryan J. *California and Its Missions.* San Francisco, 1904.

Engelbert, Omer. *The Last of the Conquistadors.* Harcourt Brace, 1956.

Engelhardt, Charles A., O.F.M. *Mission San Carlos Borromeo.* Santa Barbara, 1934.

Missions and Missionaries of California. San Francisco, 1908.

Geiger, Maynard, O.F.M. *The Life and Times of Junipero Serra.* A.A.F.H., Washington, D.C., 1959.

Mission Bells of Santa Barbara. Santa Barbara.

Harte, Bret. *The Angelus Bells.*

Helm, McKinley. *Fray Junipero Serra, The Great Walker.* Stanford University Press, 1956.

Manning, Timothy. *The Grey Ox.* Paterson, New Jersey, 1948.

Maynard, Theodore. *The Long Road of Father Serra.* Appleton-Century-Crofts, 1954.

McRoskey, Racine. *The Missions of California.* San Francisco, 1914.

Palou, Francisco. *Relacion Historica de la Vida y Apostolicas Tareas Del Venerable Padre Fray Junipero Serra.* (Trans.-George Wharton James) Pasadena, 1913.

The Founding of the First California Missions. (Trans. - Douglas S. Watson) San Francisco, 1934.

Parkes, Henry Bamford. *A History of Mexico.* Boston, 1960.

Prescott, William H. *Conquest of Mexico.* New York, 1843.

Priestley, Herbert I. *The Mexican Nation: A History.* New York, 1923.

Repplier, Agnes. *Junipero Serra, Pioneer Colonist of California.* Garden City, 1933.

Tibesar, Antonini, O.F.M. (Editor). *Writings of Junipero Serra.* A.A.F.H., Washington, D.C., 1955.

Woodgate, M. V. *Junipero Serra, Apostle of California.* Newman Press, 1966.

Index

228